COACHING KIDS SOCCER

AGES 5 TO 10

VOLUME 3

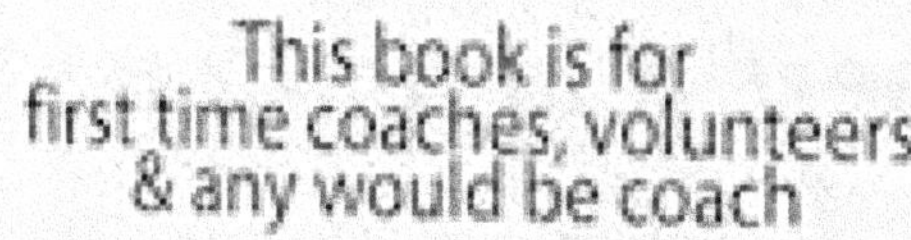

This book is for
first time coaches, volunteers
& any would be coach

Set up simple, fun and effective drills &
organise a practice session in 5 minutes!

CHRIS KING

COACHING KIDS SOCCER

AGES 5 TO 10 - VOLUME 3

20 FUN SOCCER DRILLS THAT TEACH SOCCER SKILLS TO 5 TO 10 YEAR OLDS PLUS GENERAL COACHING ADVICE

This book is for amateur grassroots coaches, volunteers and parents.

After reading this book you will be able to run a kids soccer training session with confidence!

This book is aimed at coaching 5 to 10 year olds soccer. It has 20 soccer games that will help improve the four main aspects that kids should focus on in their early development:

1. Passing
2. Dribbling
3. Shooting
4. 1v1

You can choose any of the games from this book to use at training and they will improve at least one (if not all four!) of those skills.

You will also learn how to structure a kids training session using the games from this book that develop soccer skills while at the same time making sure the kids have lots of fun!

So let's jump into it.

HOW TO STRUCTURE A KIDS TRAINING SESSION

Here is how I layout a kids training session.

I would encourage you to structure your training session the same as I have below.

Children like some structure. So if you follow the session layout you will find that children soon get to know what to do as the season progresses, which makes training easier for them and coaching more enjoyable for you.

(Note: If you also coach youth and adult teams, my book **"Training Sessions For Soccer Coaches Book 1"** lays out how to structure training sessions for youth and adult teams as well as which drills to use).

My training sessions are split into 5 Parts. So whatever amount of time you have, simply divide the time into 5 and spend equal amounts of time on each part. Easy! (Note: Allow 10 minutes for talking and explaining drills throughout the session).

PRE TRAINING: SMALL SIDED GAME	PART 1: ESSENTIAL SKILL PRACTISE	PART 2: FUN GAME	PART 3: SMALL SIDED GAME (with slight change)	PART 4: FUN GAME	PART 5: SMALL SIDED GAME
Kids go straight into a game as they start arriving at training.	Practise a skill that will be the focus of the session. (ie Passing; Dribbling; 1v1; Shooting)	Fun games related to soccer. A chance for kids to spend time on the ball & experience success.	3v3 up to 5v5 on a small pitch with goals. Encourage the main skill that is the focus of the session.	Fun games related to soccer. A chance for kids to spend time on the ball & experience success.	3v3 up to 5v5 on a small pitch with goals.

Okay let's get started by explaining the first section…

PRE-TRAINING: SMALL SIDED GAME - Use this as children arrive at training up until the official training start time.

This is a great way to start the session before it's actually started! As kids turn up, simply get them straight into a game! There might be at least a 15 minute gap between the first child arriving and training actually starting, so why waste this time? Get them into a game and this helps them get extra touches on the ball and improve their soccer skills before training has even started.

As kids turn up, give them a bib and let them loose in a game! Parents can join in to make up the numbers to start with.

1. Have 1 or 2 small fields marked out (approx 20x15 metres). I know you may only have limited space if you are waiting for other teams to finish training but try and find a small area somewhere.

2. Organise the children into 2 teams as they turn up (have two sets of bibs on the ground ready to go). Try to keep it to a maximum of 4 or 5 a side so that all the players are getting plenty of touches. If there are more than 8-10 players, get another game going in the next square.

3. Simply throw a ball in the middle and away they go! Now they are having fun and getting better at soccer before training has even started!

PART 1: ESSENTIAL SKILL PRACTISE - This is the time where we want the children to get lots of touches on the ball and work on their essential/fundamental skills.

Get them all to grab a ball and then show and tell them what skill they will be working on in this training session.

If it's with really young players, it may just be showing them how to do Toe Taps or Sol Rolls. If this is the case, show and tell them how to do it and get them straight into it (they learn by doing)! Then you can go around as they practise and help them out individually.

Stop them after a minute or two and re-show them and get one of the kids to show everyone the skill as well.

If they are older players you may be working on Turns or Passing. If this is the case, in the following Parts (Part 2 through to Part 5) try to make sure to emphasise and encourage Turns or Passing as they play.

PART 2: FUN GAME - A fun game related to soccer. This is a chance for kids to spend time on the ball and experience success.

Use any drill from this book or my previous two (Coaching Kids Soccer Volume 1 and Coaching Kids Soccer Volume 2). Make sure to put emphasis on one main skill that you are working on in this session (ie Passing; Dribbling; Shooting; 1v1).

PART 3: SMALL SIDED GAME (with a slight change) - Play 3v3 up to 5v5 on a small pitch with goals (any more than 5v5, set up another pitch so players get plenty of touches). During the game make sure to encourage the main skill that is the focus of the session (ie Passing; Dribbling; Shooting; 1v1).

TIP: You can do this by awarding double goals if the skill is performed in the lead up to the goal. **For example, if you are working on passing for this session, make the slight change that if a team makes 5 passes before scoring a goal, they get awarded 2 goals.**

PART 4: FUN GAME - The same as Part 1, this is another fun game related to soccer. This is another chance for kids to spend time playing soccer, improve their skills and experience success.

Use any drill from this book or my previous two (Coaching Kids Soccer Volume 1 and Coaching Kids Soccer Volume 2)

PART 5: SMALL SIDED GAME - Back to playing a game! 3v3 up to 5v5 on a small pitch with goals. Don't make any rule changes here. Simply encourage them to have fun and allow the kids to explore playing against each other. Let them learn by doing!

So that is how to structure your training session. Fairly easy isn't it?

Before getting into the fun soccer games that I've put together for you, here are a few things to keep in mind when training young children (make sure to reread these points every couple of weeks so they stay front of mind):

- You will have kids with different levels of skill and experience, so make sure to **encourage and praise all the players** - not just the ones that are at a better skill level. They all develop at a different rate.

- Create opportunities where **all the children can experience success (ie a drill where everyone gets to score a goal or work on a skill and improve it).**

- **Be patient** and give them time to grasp what you are showing them (make sure to demonstrate skills - kids pick things up easier by observing than just listening to an explanation).

- Use games that encourage **every child to have a ball at their feet as much as possible.**

- **Praise each child for their effort,** no matter what the end result.

- **Keep the children excited!** Act like a clown or be over enthusiastic if you need to be.

- **Use simple language** to explain things and make sure to demonstrate the skill or drill.

- **Encourage players to be creative.**

- **Keep it fun** so they will want to come back next time.

PRE-PRACTICE TIPS FOR THE COACH
- Arrive early so your games/areas are set up.

- As mentioned in the Training Session Structure, when the children start arriving, organise them into a game straight away.

- Enjoy the session! Forget about anything else that is happening in your life and just enjoy coaching the children.

EQUIPMENT NEEDED (IF POSSIBLE)
- 1 ball per child
- 12 cones (approximately)
- 2 or 4 mini goals (use poles or cones if no goals)
- 4 sets of different coloured bibs

SETTING UP
If you're not sure exactly how many children you will have for the session, it's best to set up an extra 'mirror drill' (two of the same drill) just in case.

I like to set the two areas up side by side with a channel in the middle where I can see both areas and therefore keep an eye on everything. Plus I can distribute balls to both areas.

Tip: *You can lose children's attention very quickly, so by having everything set up as much as possible ahead of time and therefore not* *having to stop to set up during a session, it leads to the kids not getting distracted and a smoothly run session.*

Use the same coloured cones for one pitch and a different set of coloured cones for the other. This is so it is clear to the children which pitch is which. (Then, for example, you can say to them "Team 1 and 2 on the pitch with yellow cones" and they know where to go straight away).

See the images below for how I set up (this example has 12 children with two 3v3 games) and then we'll get into the fun soccer games!

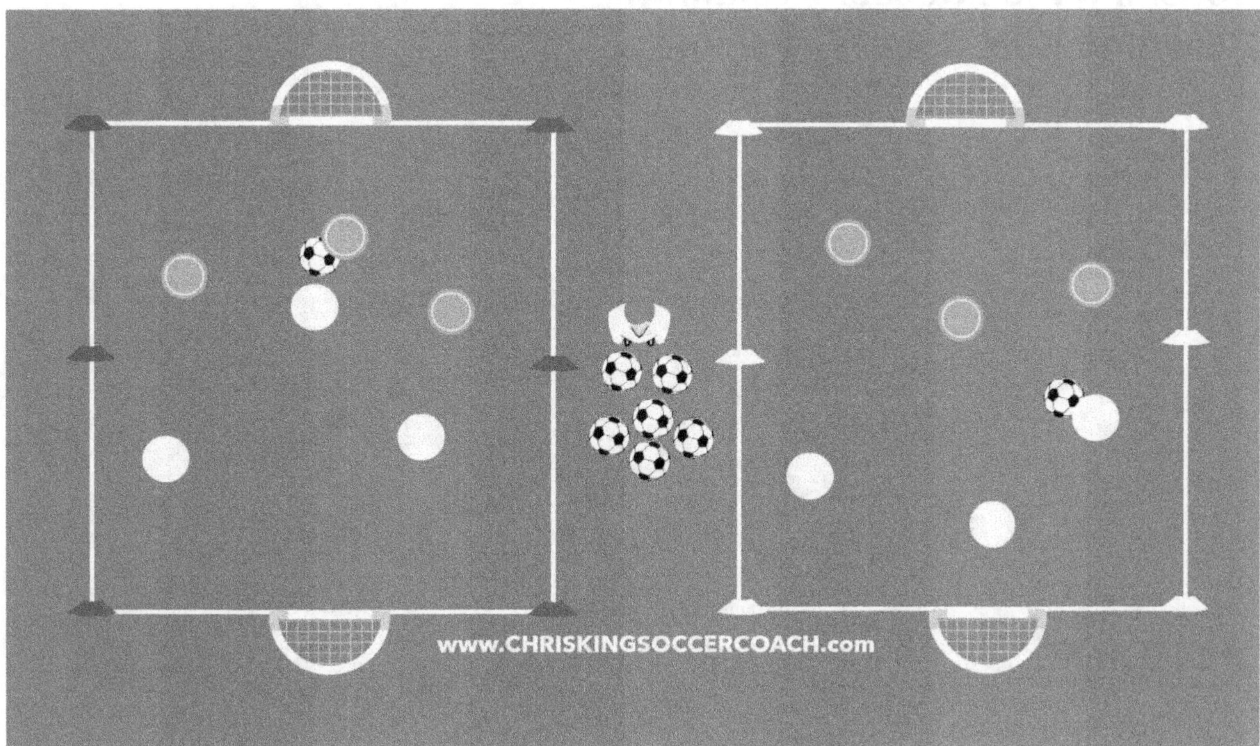

This is how I set up my games and position myself if I have two small areas. I can keep an eye on both and distribute balls to both pitches.

Happy Coaching!
Chris King

Chris King

Sign up at www.chriskingsoccercoach.com for free drills and soccer tips.

Other soccer books by Chris King available on Amazon. Visit his website at www.chriskingsoccercoach.com

Coaching Kids Soccer - Volume 1
Coaching Kids Soccer - Volume 2

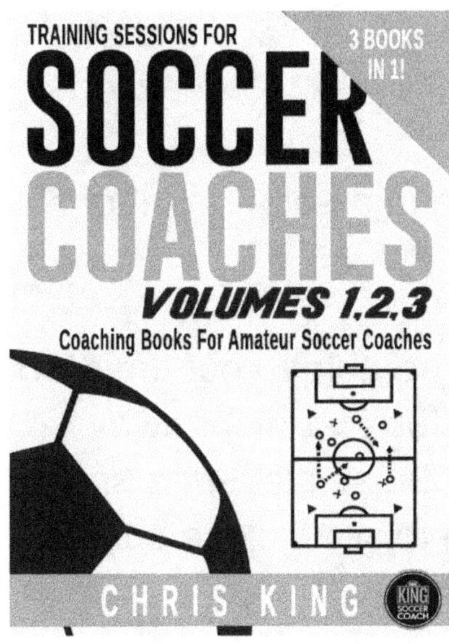

20 FUN SOCCER DRILLS

GAME #1
"POLES"

FOCUS OF SESSION:

This is a simple but effective drill. "Poles" help kids with their dribbling skills, getting their head up to scan the area, changing direction with the ball and keeping close possession.

SET UP:

- **4 to 12 players**
- 25x25 yard square
- 6 Poles

THE DRILL:

In a large square, randomly spread poles around the area. Players start inside the square with a ball each.

They must dribble around as many poles as they can in a set amount of time (usually 1 minute), avoiding other players.

After 1 minute, call out "Stop" and all players should be able to put their foot on the ball. If the ball is too far away and they can't stop it straight away, this means the player hasn't kept close control. Give those players a small task to do (5 toe taps on the ball) to encourage them to keep close control next time.

Ask how many poles each player got around in the minute. Then see if they can improve on their next round.

Call out different parts of the foot to use (ie "Soles only!" "Outside of the foot only" "Right foot only!). This all helps their development and confidence.

COACHES NOTES:

- Players should have close control so that in a game defenders can't steal the ball from them. Every now and then, walk around the square and lightly kick the kids' balls if the ball is too far from their body. This shows them how a Defender could steal it.

- Players should be regularly looking around so they can see where the next pole is and so they can avoid the other players.

CHANGE IT:

Encourage personal improvement - for example, can they get around 6 poles in 1 minute the first go? Then the next minute can they beat their last attempt and get around 8?

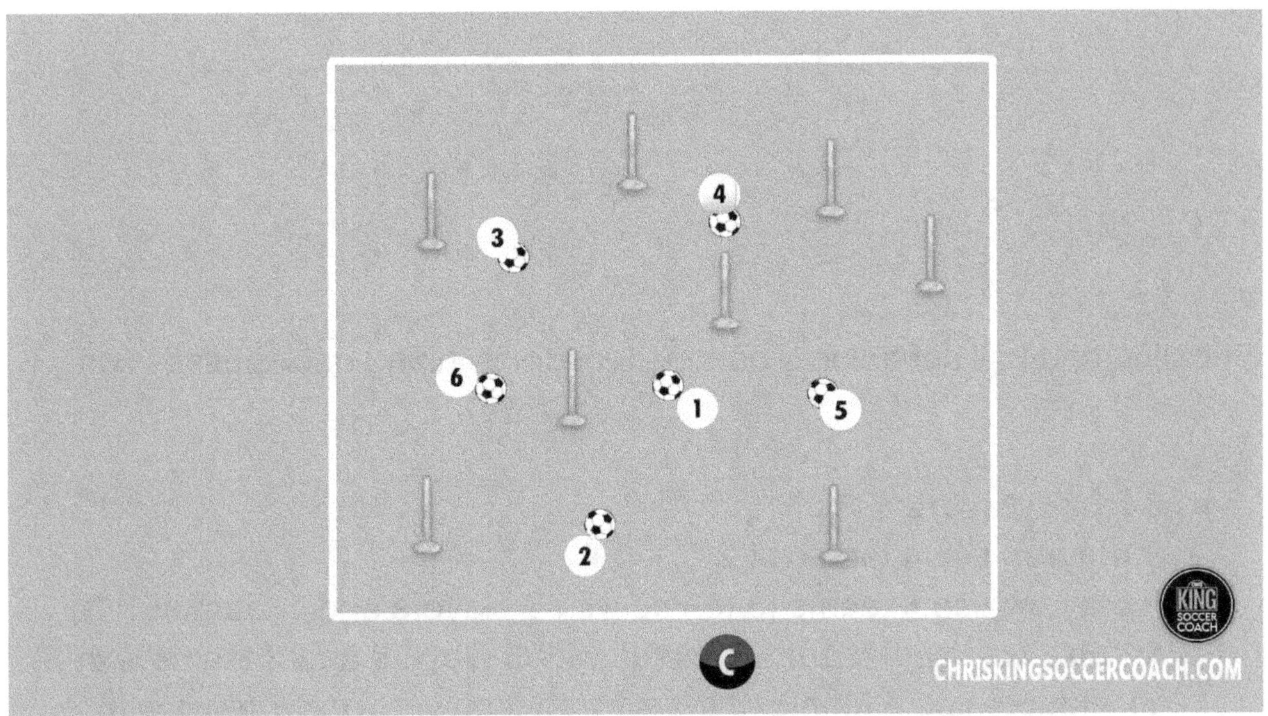

Each player starts with a ball. When the coach calls out "Go!" players try to get around as many poles as they can.

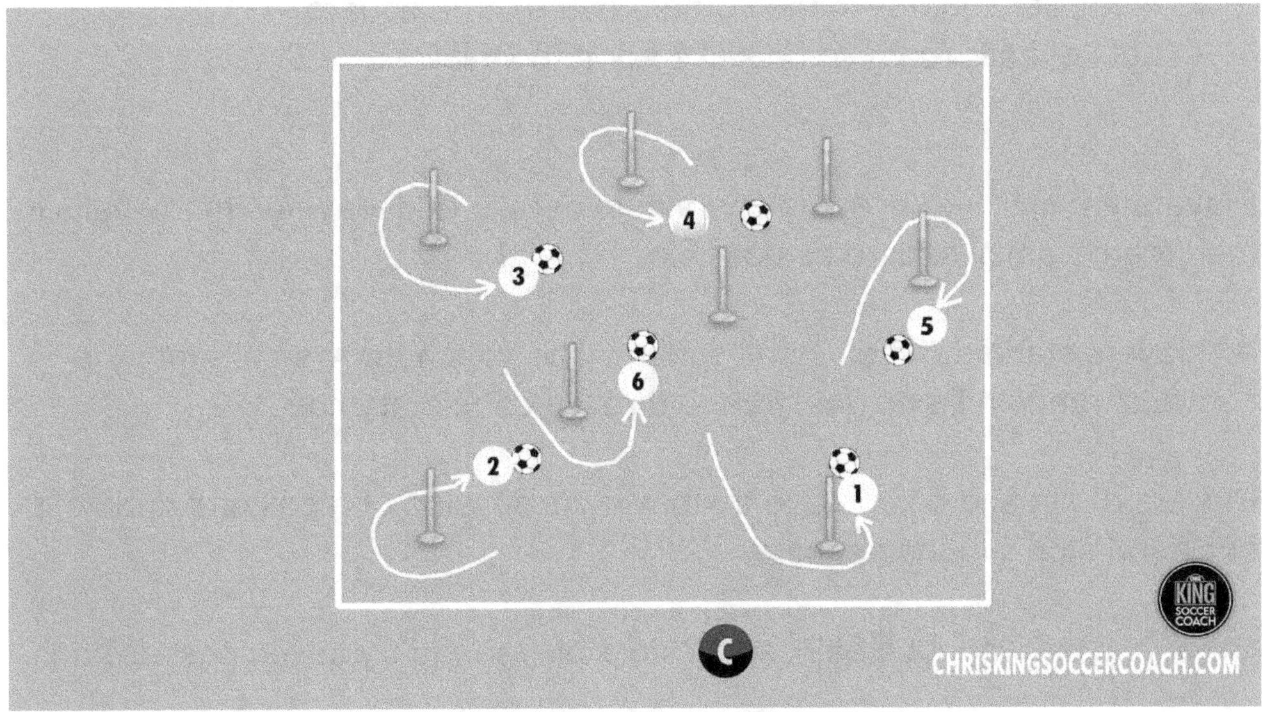

Players must keep close control and get their heads up so they don't run into other players or balls. In the above image, #4's ball is a bit too far from them and the ball could be stolen in a game situation.

GAME #2
"MOST BALLS WINS"

⬤ FOCUS OF SESSION:

Dribbling and ball control in a game situation. Winning back possession.

◼ SET UP:

- **8 to 12 players**
  8 players use 4 teams of 2
  9 players use 4 teams (3 teams with 2 players and 1 team with 3)
  10 players use 4 teams (2 teams with 3 players and 2 teams with 2)
  11 players use 4 teams (3 teams with 3 players and 1 team with 2)
  12 players use 4 teams with 3 players.
- 25x25 yard square
- 4 smaller squares in the corners of the large square
- Lots of balls ready to be kicked or thrown in!

THE DRILL:

Players are split into 4 teams and aim to dribble and leave as many balls in their team's small square as possible.

All players start near their small square. The coach throws balls into the centre at random times (feel free to throw a couple at once).

Players run in and compete to try to win possession of a ball and dribble it back and stop it in their square.

Other players without a ball can tackle a player and try to win possession.

Once all the balls are in the small squares, count up who has the most and that team wins!

- Having the players stop the ball in the square helps with their close control. Players shouldn't be just kicking and chasing the ball with the balls going way past their square. Make sure to give a demonstration before starting on how close control dribbling looks and how to stop the ball. (Lots of little touches with the feet so the ball isn't too far ahead and stop it with the sole of the foot).

- Make sure to throw and roll the balls in at different speeds and heights so players are practising different control techniques.

- Try and get the players to concentrate. If they don't have a ball make sure they are looking around to either try and win possession off an opponent or they are ready for when the coach throws a new ball in.

#1 - Join two teams together so, for example, there would be 4v4 in an 8 player game.

#2 - Use different skills while dribbling - i.e. players must use just their left foot or players must perform a sole roll while dribbling back.

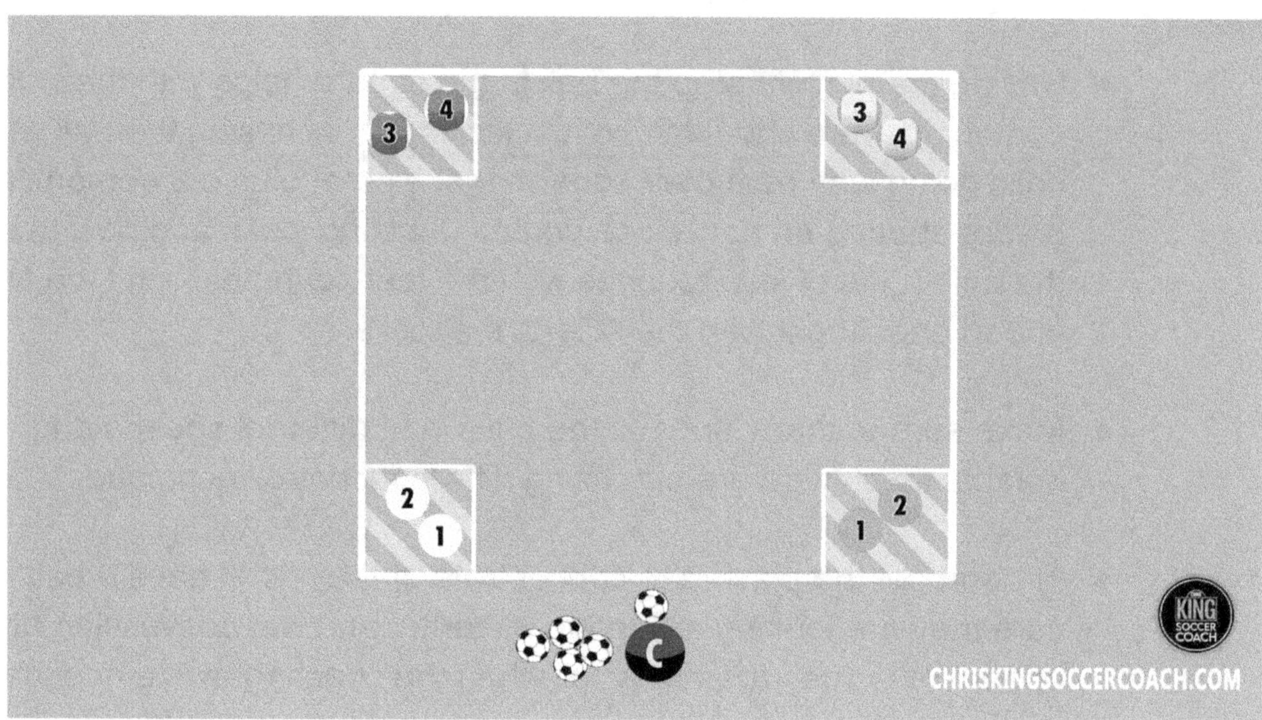

Players start in their small squares with the coach ready to throw some balls in.

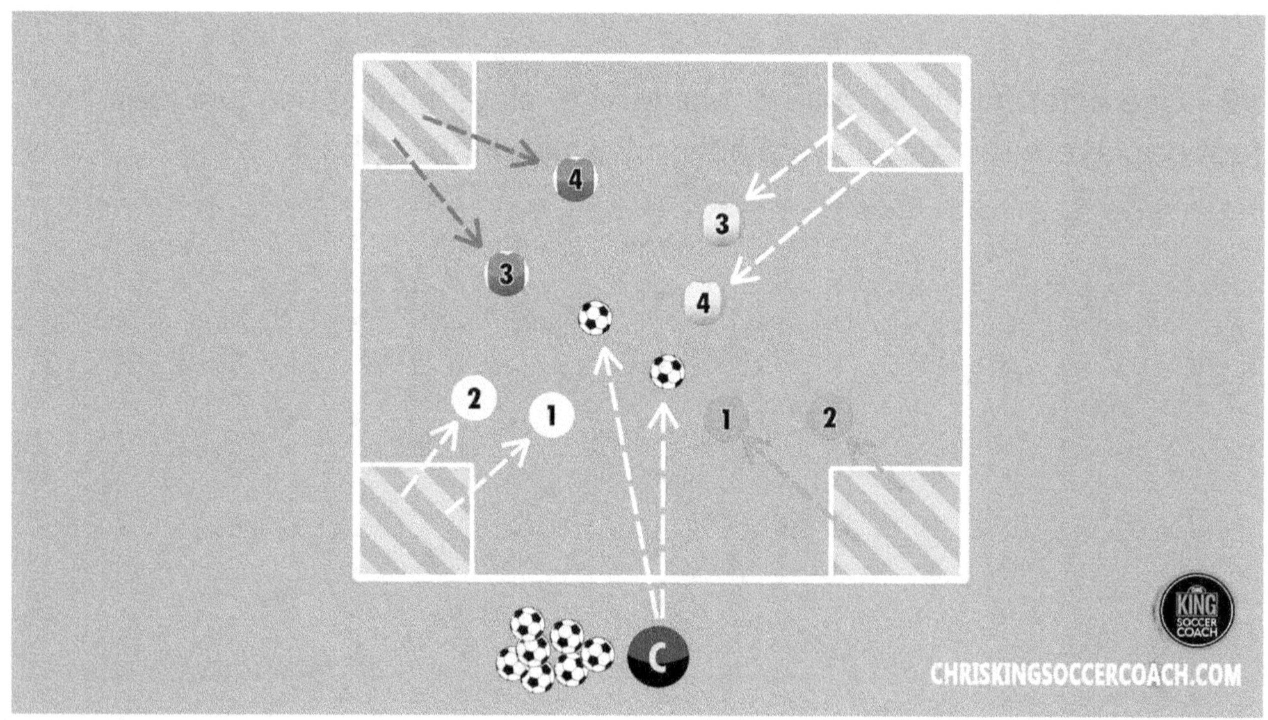

As soon as the balls are kicked/thrown in, players can run in and compete to win the ball.

Here Dark #3 has won a ball and dribbled it back to their square and stopped it. Light #1 and Darkish #1 are competing for a ball.
Play until all balls have been dribbled into a small square and count up how many each team has. The most balls win.

GAME #3
"SANTA/PARTY HATS"

● FOCUS OF SESSION:

Getting the players to have fun while getting used to a game situation. Players will use all four main skills: Dribbling, Passing, 1v1, Shooting.

<u>Note:</u> This drill can be adjusted for anytime of the year, not just Christmas! Simply swap the Santa hats for party hats, pirate hats, regular caps (get the kids to bring their own!) etc.

- **4 to 12 players**
  (either 2v2, 3v3, 4v4, 5v5 or 6v6)
- Small 20x15 yard pitch with small goals at each end
- Split the players into two teams
- Have Santa hats ready for players to put on

THE DRILL:

Simple! Regular soccer rules but each time a team scores, one player gets to put a Santa hat on.

Once every player on a team has a Santa hat on that team wins!

COACHES NOTES:

- A game situation like this uses all aspects of soccer - communication, movement, plus all different skills (passing, dribbling, taking players on 1v1, shooting). So players will naturally be working on different skills.

  But every now and then bring in a restriction for two minutes to help them focus on one particular skill.

  For example, make restrictions such as:

1. There must be three passes before a goal can be scored.
2. A player must dribble past an opponent before a goal can be scored.
3. All players must touch the ball before a goal can be scored.

This helps to work on different skills but also helps them to communicate and concentrate on the task at hand.

CHANGE IT:

#1 - If a player can name three of Santa's reindeers they get an extra Santa hat.

#2 - If a player can spell "reindeer or Christmas" they get an extra hat.

#3 - I think you can see where this is going. See if you can come up with some other fun, Christmasy ones.

Ho! Ho! Ho!

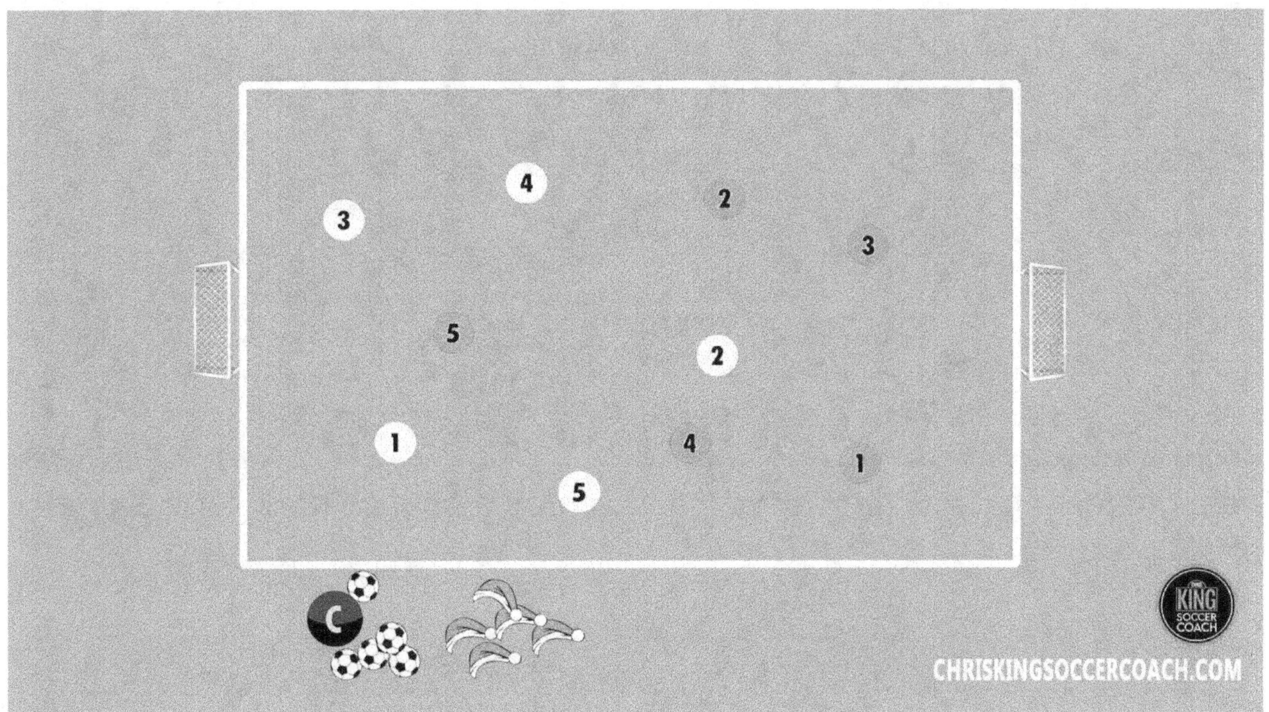

Players are ready for action. Who can be the first team to score 5 goals and get a Santa hat for every player?

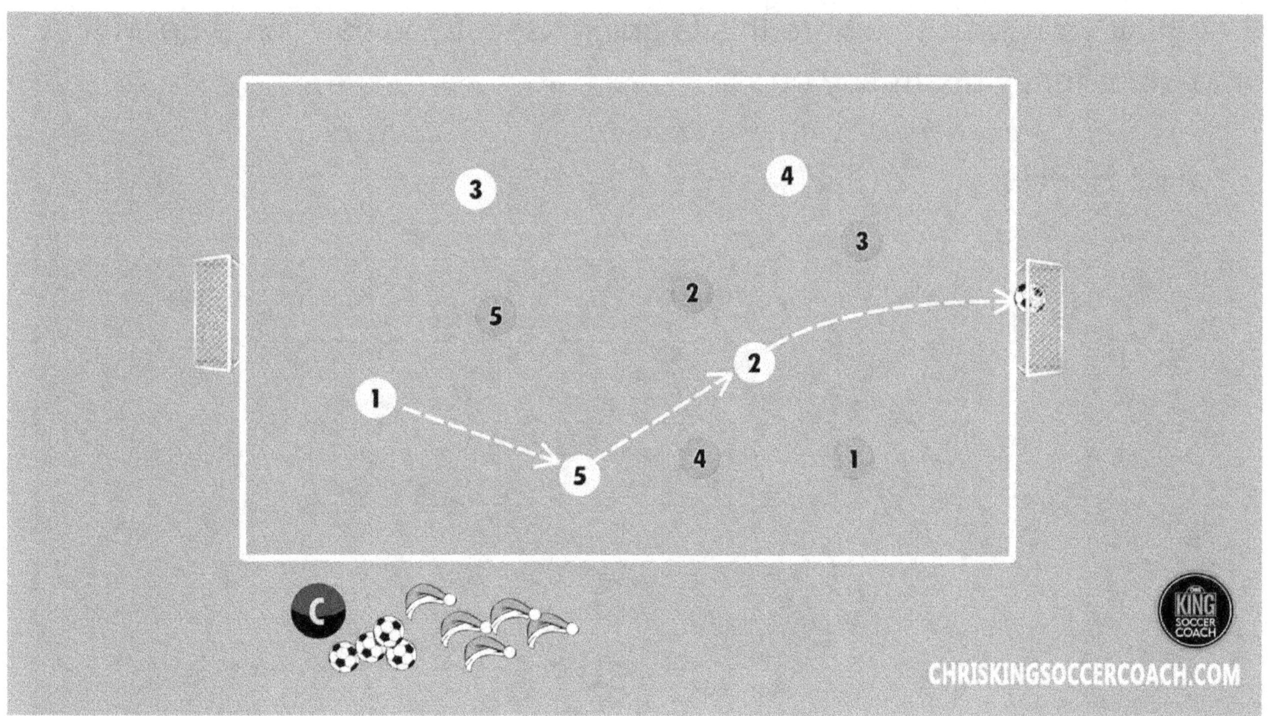

The Light team passes the ball well and scores a goal so they get a Santa hat.

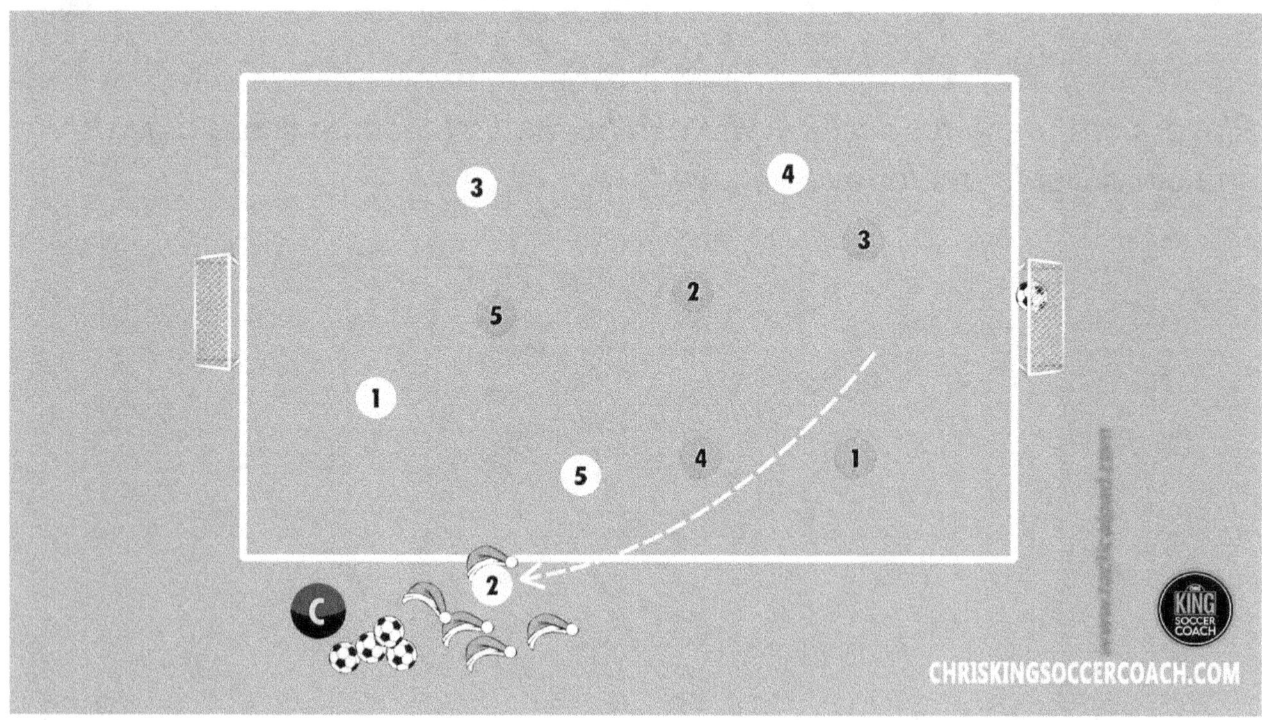

Light #2 puts it on and everyone keeps playing until one team has all their players in a Santa hat.

GAME #4
"BIBS"

● FOCUS OF SESSION:

This drill helps with young players' basic and fundamental movement skills. At an early age, players are still learning what their bodies can do. So in this drill they will get to develop speed, change of direction and spatial awareness.

■ SET UP:

- **5 to 16 players**
- 25 yard circle
- A bib for every player

THE DRILL:

Sometimes called "Tails", "Bibs" simply involves each player tucking a bib into the back of their shorts (so it looks like they have a tail).

Note: Make sure that half the bib is in and half is out otherwise you will get some players tucking 95% of it in their shorts so other players can't get it!

Before starting the actual game, get all players to start by moving around the circle, dodging this way and that, turning and moving in all directions. They are just getting used to avoiding each other, faking out each other, quick changes of direction etc. At this stage you can call out a few instructions if you wish (i.e. faster, left, backwards, etc), otherwise just let them run and move.

Once the coach shouts "Go!' all the players must try and steal each other's bibs out from the back of their shorts. Their aim is to try and win as many as possible (they hold the bibs they win in their hands)!

After 1 minute (or once everyone has had their bib stolen), shout "Stop!" and players count up how many bibs they grabbed. The player with the most gets a high five from the coach! ● Or they get to shout "I am the best Bib player in the world!!!" (Similar to Billy Madison in his spelling bee contest).

- **Changes of speed!** I can't mention this enough. A quick burst of speed can soon get a player out of trouble. Teach the players to get in the habit of exploding away when they decide to change directions.

- **Faking!** Teach the players to do an exaggerated step one way (which will unbalance a defender in a game) and then go the other way. The same with a shoulder drop - get the players to drop their shoulder as if they were going one way and then get them to move off in the opposite direction.

  Note: In a game situation, a good deceptive tactic is raising an arm as if you are getting ready to shoot. The defender sees this and subconsciously puts out their leg to block the shot/long pass or they stop to put their body or leg in the way. When this happens the Attacker can go past them.

- **Look around!** Teach the players to get their heads up whenever they can. This will feel unnatural in their early development when they are still learning skills. But it will become easier as they get more familiar with the ball. Looking around helps with knowing where to pass, what spaces to move/dribble into and where the opposition and teammates are.

#1 - Players dribble a ball as they try to steal bibs!

#2 - Split the players into teams and players work as a team to try to get all the other teams bibs. First team to get all the other teams' bibs wins!

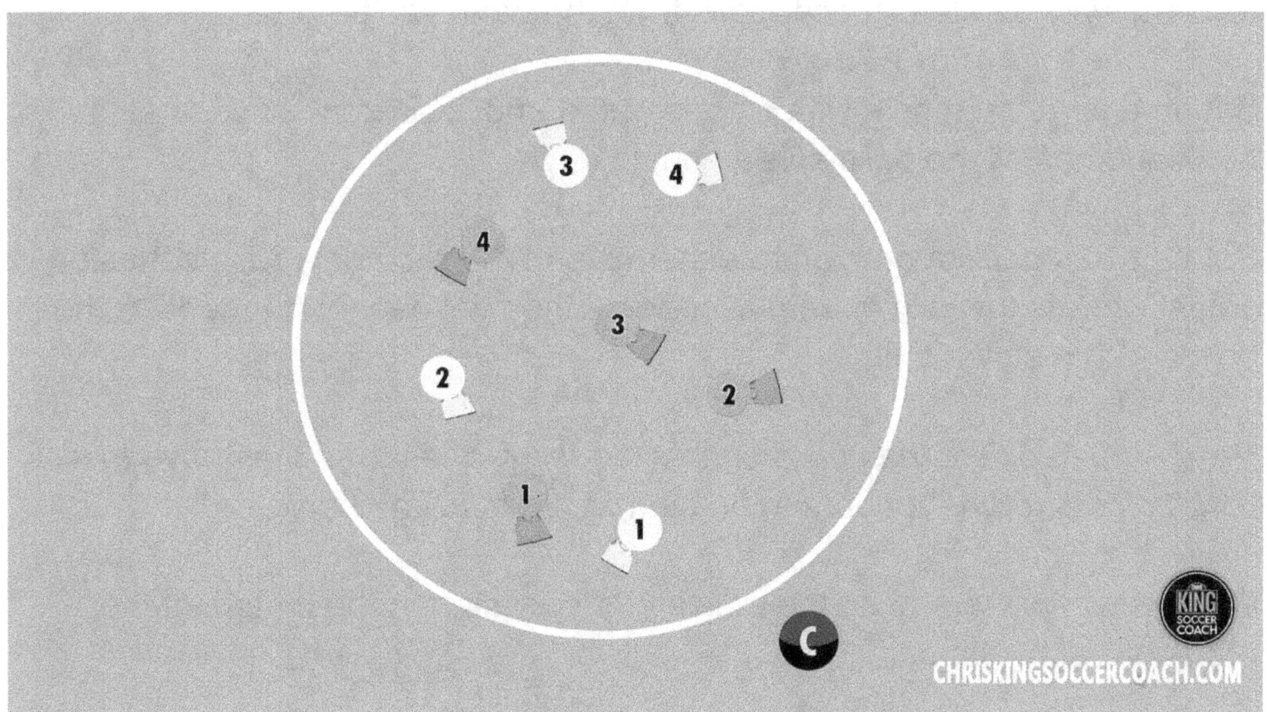

All players start with a bib tucked into the back of their shorts. Play until all the bibs have been taken and then count up who got the most.

GAME #5
"BANK ROBBERS"

FOCUS OF SESSION:

Dribbling, passing and evasive skills.

SET UP:

- **6 to 18 players**
- 30x20 yard rectangle with 2 small squares off to either side
- 2 bibs
- Lots of balls

THE DRILL:

This drill is lots of fun! Two police (in bibs) against a whole lot of little bank robbers trying to steal soccer balls from the bank vault!

Set up a large rectangle with a zone at the end. This zone is used as a bank and has all the balls spread out in it.

Set up two small squares off to either side of the rectangle (use cones or poles) - this is the jail where players go if they get caught (tagged) by the police with a stolen ball.

Note: *You decide if the police simply tag the robbers or if they have to kick their ball out for the robbers to be caught on their way back.*

Choose two players to be the police and they start in the middle of the rectangle with bibs on.

Get the other players to pair up and they start at the opposite end to the bank.

One player from each pair races into the middle and tries to make it to the bank without getting caught (tagged) by the police! If they get caught they run back to their partner and let them have a turn at robbing the bank.

If they are successful at getting to the bank, they get a ball and try to get it back to their partner without getting tagged. They can either dribble or pass it back to their partner.

But if they get caught (tagged) by the police on their way back they have to return their ball to the bank, go to jail (either of the two small squares to the side) and do 5 jumping jacks. Their partner can go while they are in jail.

As soon as all the balls have been successfully stolen from the bank, count up the balls to see which pair has the most money (each ball is worth 1 000 000 pounds!).

- To avoid being caught by the police, are the players using: Change of speed? Quick change of direction? Body feints (dropping the shoulder or stepping one way and going the other)? All this helps in their development of body movement.

- Are the players using both dribbling and passing to get the ball back to their partner? There is no right or wrong here. As long as they are trying both they will improve their decision making on when to dribble past an opponent and when to pass. If there is an obvious, easy pass back to their partner, they should get in the habit of passing. As my old coach used to say, "It's quicker to pass a ball to your teammate than to dribble it to them".

- Are the police (the Defenders) shepherding a robber towards one side so they don't have as many options to get past them? Also, the Defenders shouldn't rush in full steam because the robbers can then just pick a side and go past. Instead they should jockey a little bit and pick their moment to tag the robber.

◼ CHANGE IT:

#1 - Add more police or remove a police officer depending on numbers or skill levels of the players. Or make the Coach the police officer! I often like to make myself the Defender in a drill and that way I can coach and encourage the kids while I'm out amongst them.

#2 - Give the players bibs to tuck into their shorts and the police have to grab the bib for the robber to be caught! And make it so if the police grab 5 bibs they win and every robber has to do 10 jumping jacks.

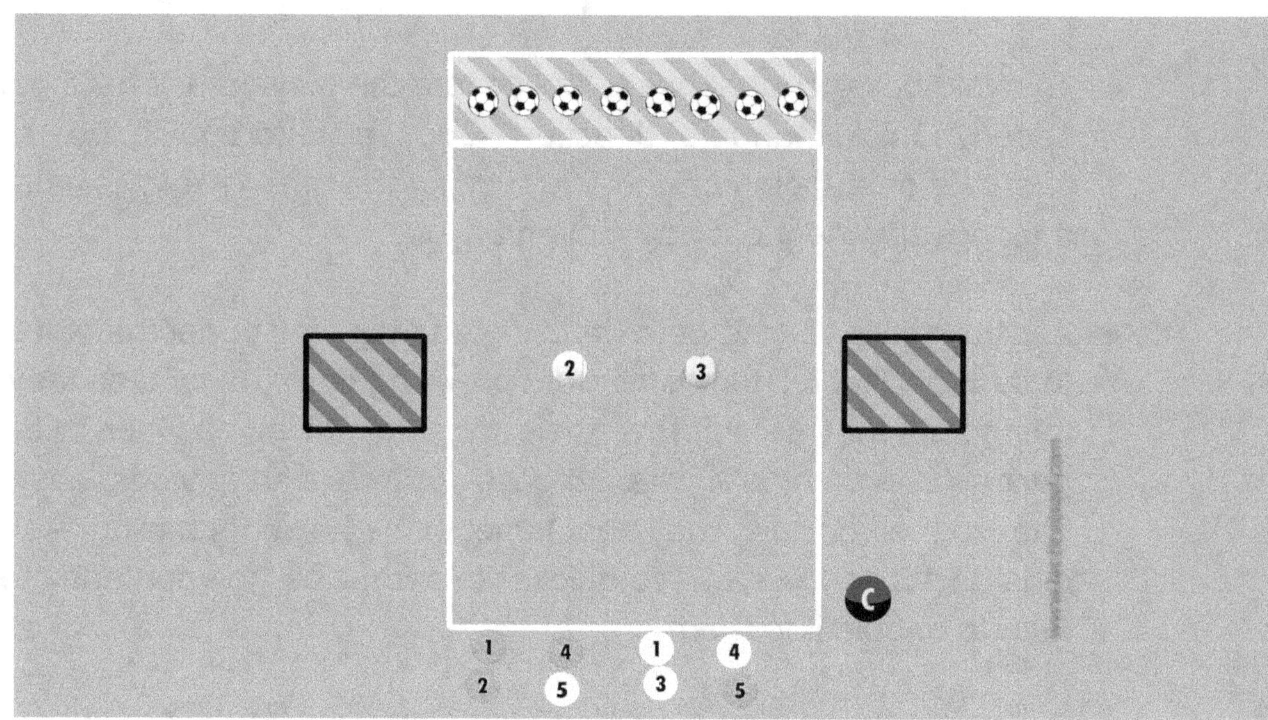

Two police start in the middle (White #2 and #3). The bank robbers start at the bottom, ready to try and get past the police and steal a ball from the bank!

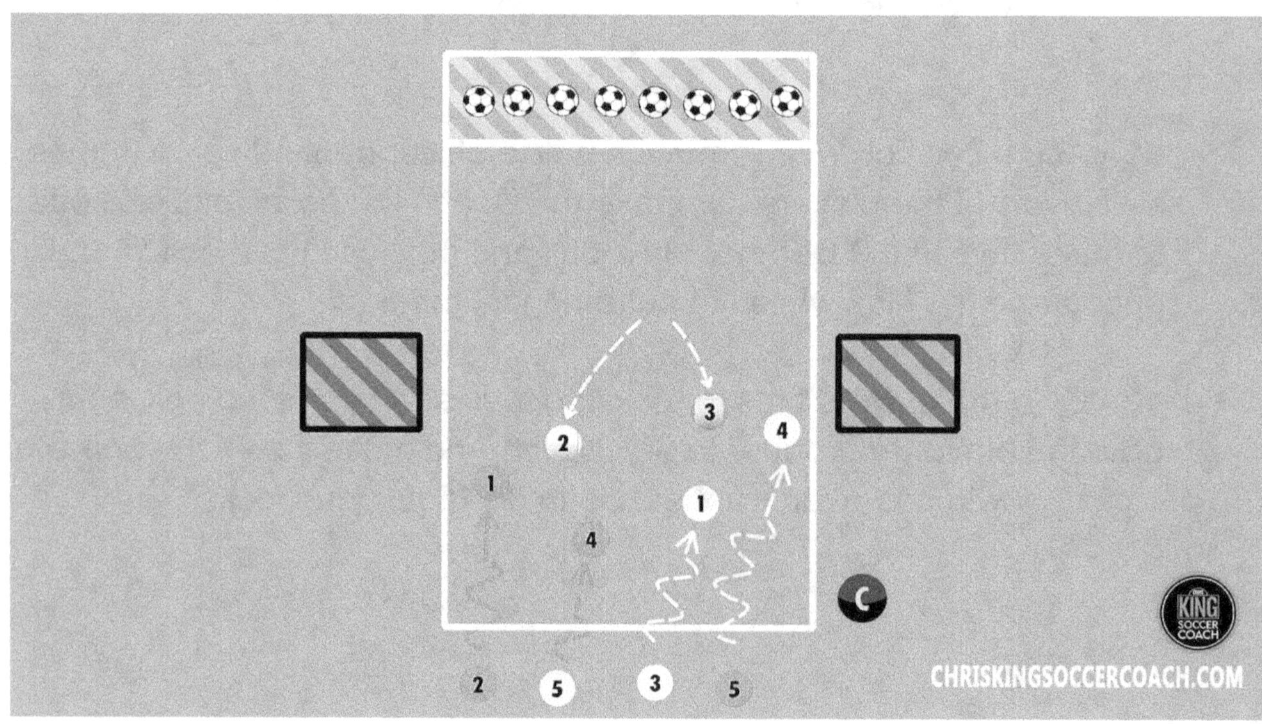

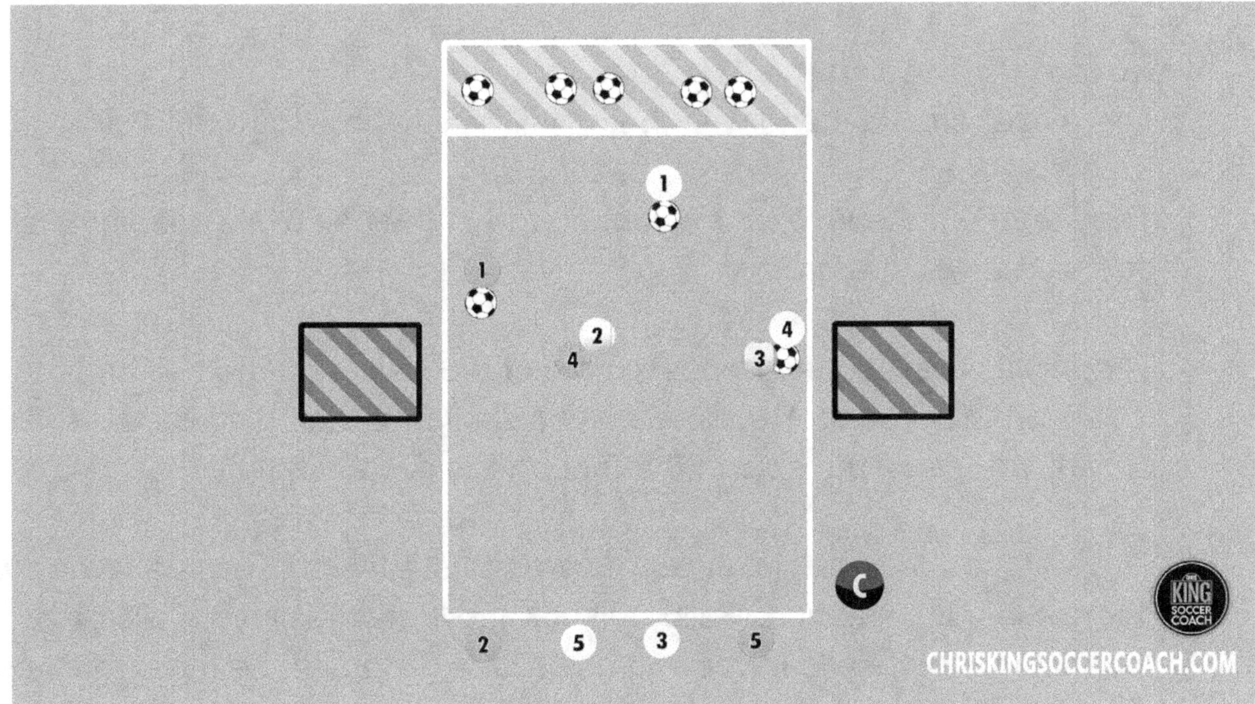

Dark and Light #1's made it to the bank and are on the way back to their partner. Dark #4 got caught by the Police (#2) and must return and let their partner have a try. Light #4 got caught with a ball so must return it to the bank vault and go to jail and perform 5 jumping jacks.

<u>INTERMISSION</u>

Now is a good time to explain three of the basic skills that kids will be using in the next drill. Toe Taps, Sole Rolls and Happy Feet are all footwork skills that help build a young players' touch on the ball.

Also, a bit of "beginner juggling" helps with controlling the ball at different heights and with different parts of the body.

TOE TAPS

Toe Taps are simply touches on the top of the ball using the sole of the shoe. They help improve coordination, improve players quickness of feet and improve their touch on the ball.

How to do Toe Taps:
The player should stand with the ball directly in front of them.

They then put the sole of one foot on top of the ball while keeping the other one planted on the ground.

Then switch feet so the opposite sole of the foot is on the ball and the other foot is on the ground. Repeat this. (it's similar to marching on the spot except you place the sole of the foot on the ball each time).

Players should go as slowly as required to start with. Eventually they will be doing it in a fluid motion. Build up so that eventually players will be "bouncing" as they do it (moving one foot as soon as the other touches the top of the ball).

TOE TAPS

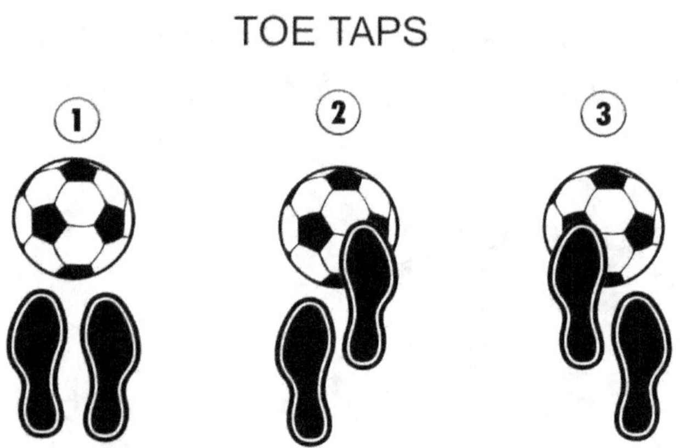

SOLE ROLLS

This helps with a players' touch and learning to move the ball.

How to do Sole Rolls:

Simply roll the ball softly *with the sole of the foot* in any direction. Then, with the same foot, roll it back to the starting position. For example, roll it out to the right with the sole of the right foot, then roll it back to the starting position with the sole of the right foot.

Start by doing it in the one spot and then progress to moving around the ground doing it.

Once they have the hang of it, players can roll it forward, backwards or whichever direction they want with the sole of either foot.

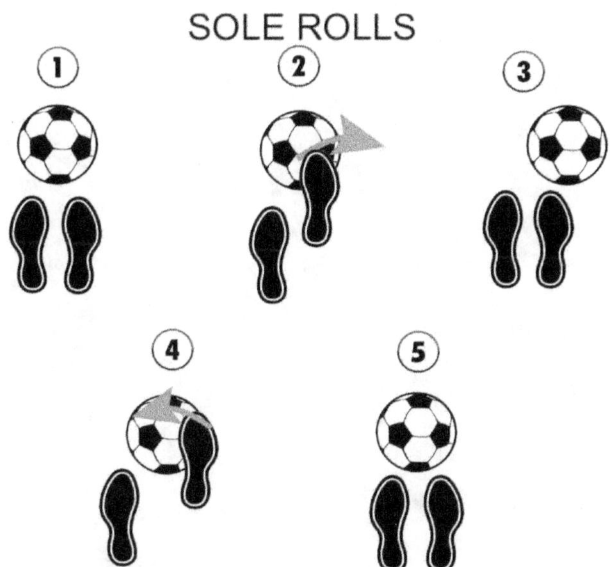

HAPPY FEET

Happy Feet are when the player is tapping the ball back and forth between the instep of their feet. Use the instep of both feet and tap it back and forth. Think of it like that old computer game "Pong".

This helps with players' touch on the ball, coordination and quick feet.

How To Do Happy Feet:
1. Start slow jogging on the spot
2. Step up to the ball and have it between the feet

3. While still slowly jogging on the spot, lightly tap the ball with the inside of your feet so the ball goes from the left foot to the right foot and back again, continuously.

Tips: Keep the head over the ball, be light on the feet and as always, start slowly until the player gets used to it.

Think of it like the old computer game Pong. This skill really helps with touch and coordination

BOUNCE JUGGLING (for beginners)

Kids don't want to become frustrated when first learning anything, so bounce juggling is a great way for players to get used to juggling without feeling like it's too hard.

It's simply allowing the ball to bounce in between every juggle (every touch) which allows them to position their body ready for the next juggle without feeling rushed.

HOW TO BOUNCE JUGGLE

1. Pick up the ball using the hands and gently throw it in the air at chest height, slightly out from the body.

2. Let the ball bounce and start to get the body in position and the foot ready to take a juggle touch.

3. Once the ball starts moving down and gets to about knee/shin height, take a touch using the top of the boot.

4. Try to kick the ball to chest/head height. This will allow enough time to get ready for the next touch (as they progress and improve they should aim to mostly kick the ball lower to the ground).

5. Get balanced so they are ready for the next touch. Let the ball bounce and then repeat!

6. Make sure to use both feet and progress to using thighs, chest and head once used to juggling with just the feet.

OK, let's get back into the games!

GAME #6
"BALL CONTROL"

● FOCUS OF SESSION:

Improve the players' ball control so they are more confident on the ball and in 1v1 situations.

■ SET UP:

- **6 to 9 players**
  (for more than 6 players adjust the size of the circle accordingly)
- Large circle
- 2 to 3 goals spread evenly around the outside of the circle (2 goals for 6 players. 3 goals for 7 to 9 players)

THE DRILL:

Players are dribbling around the circle working on their ball control (aka ball manipulation).

Firstly they use different parts of their feet: Dribbling with the insteps, dribbling with the outside of the feet, sole rolls, happy feet, toe taps, turns, etc. The coach should be calling out which skill to use.

Secondly, move onto juggling. Get the players to count how many juggles they can do and then see if they can beat their highest score. Even if it's only 1 or 2 juggles, this helps with the players being able to control the soccer ball at different heights and eventually with different parts of the body.

(**Note**: View my Coaching Kids Soccer Volume 2 book for more detailed tips on teaching young kids the art of juggling and other kids skills such as dribbling, turns, sole rolls, etc).

Thirdly, call out "Stop". Players put their foot on the ball to stop it and go and find a different ball. This helps with instant control plus it makes sure that the ball is close to them and they aren't just kicking and chasing the ball instead of dribbling.

Note: If you want, make it so the last player to stop their ball has to do 5 toe taps when they get to their new ball. Once you bring this rule in, watch as the players magically keep their ball closer than previously. Plus they will keenly listen out for your instruction to stop so as they're not the last!

Fourthly, remove half the balls and get the players to practise 1v1's in the circle. Have one player defending and the other practising shielding the ball and facing the opponent and try to get past them. Go for 45 seconds and then swap roles.

Lastly, once the players are comfortable with using different skills, juggling, stopping the ball and 1v1 situations, move onto a game within the circle where they can practise all of these skills.

Simply split the players into 2 (or 3) teams (3v3, 4v4, 4v4+1 Joker, 3v3v3 [use 3 goals]) and play a game!

- Make sure players use all parts of their feet to dribble, turn and shield the ball (inside and outside of both feet, sole rolls, etc).

- When players shield the ball, make sure to get them to use their furthest foot from the defender to control the ball. This way they have the ball under control but also it is out of reach of the defender.

- Also, when shielding the ball, can they keep their elbows up to the side of their body to make themselves bigger? I like to call this chicken wings. Call it this and the kids will remember it. And next time you say "Don't forget about your chicken wings!" watch them put their arms/elbows up beside their body to make themselves bigger and protect/shield the ball.

- Get the players to keep their head up when possible. This helps in seeing where they can pass a ball or run into space and also where the defender is coming from.

- Encourage players to take their defender on, especially if they are facing them.

- **This drill is great for the kids' confidence with ball control. They firstly get to practise the skills unopposed, then 1v1 and later on in a game situation.**

Put the coach or a parent in the circle and try to steal the players' balls. Make it exciting! Say things like "Right! Here comes the coach! I'm going to win the ball off Michael and Ingrid!" and watch those players smile, laugh and try even harder!

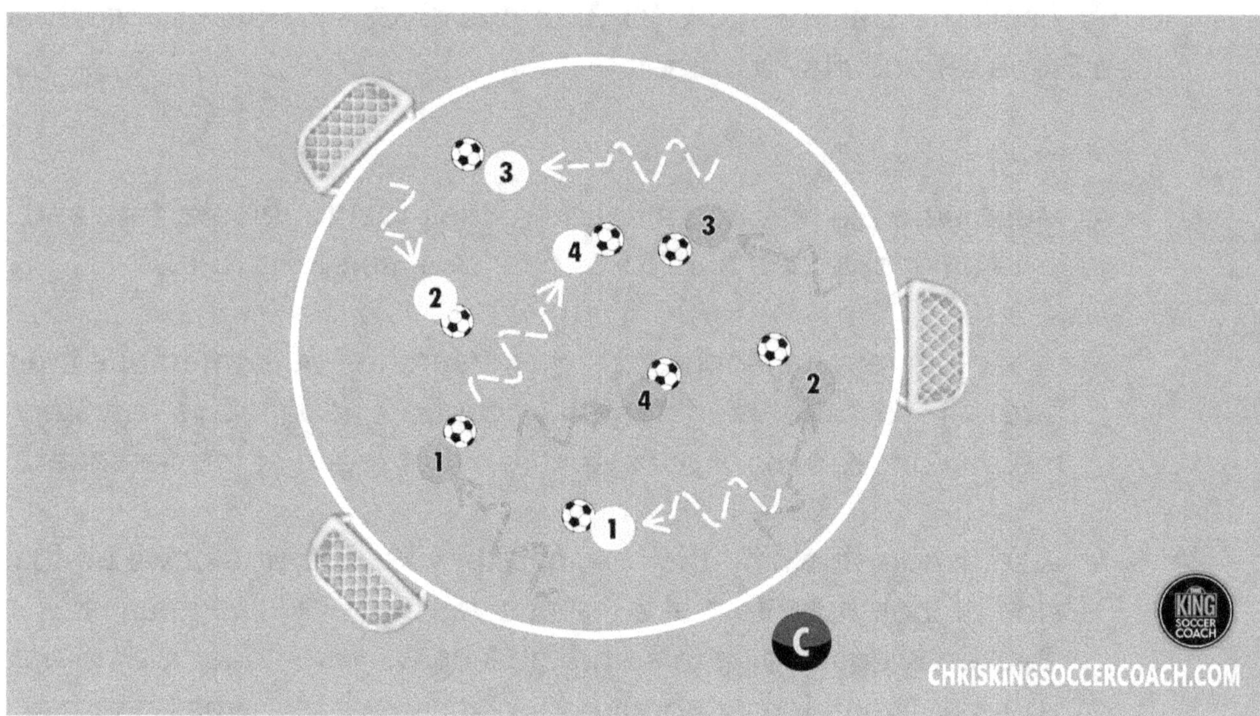

Firstly players dribble around the circle using different parts of their feet and performing different skills (insteps, sole rolls, happy feet, toe taps, turns, etc).

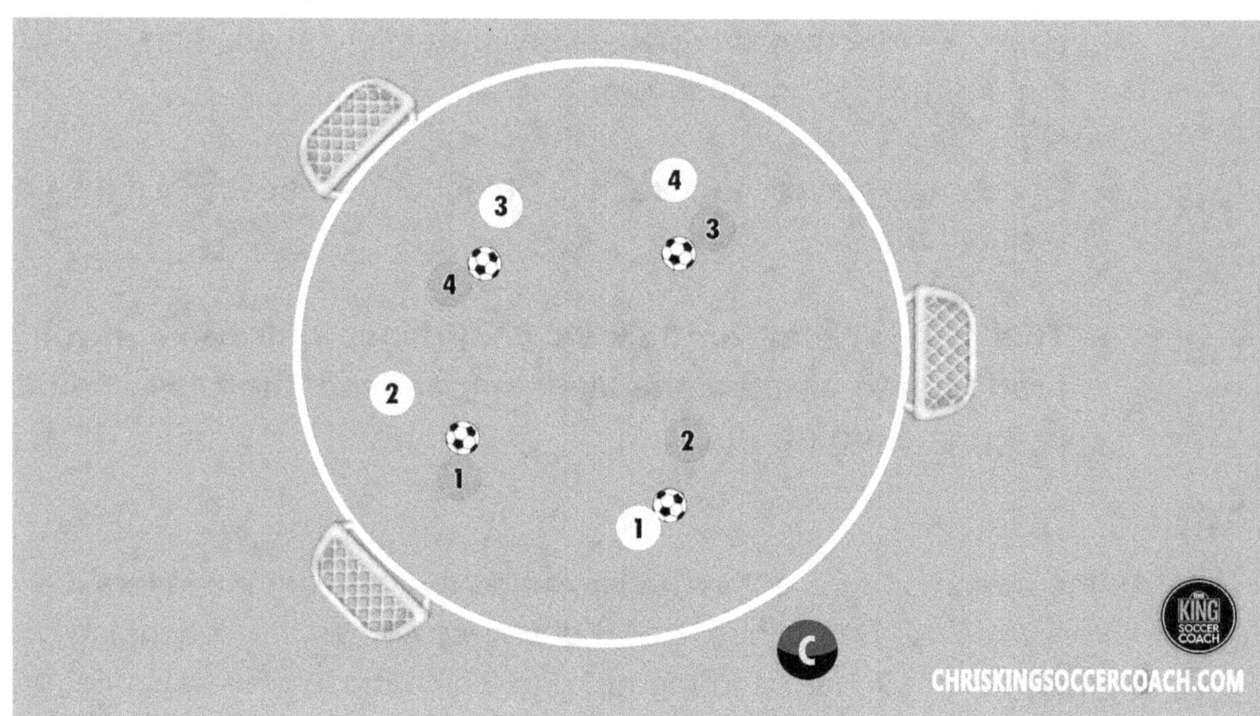

After practising a bit of juggling and stopping and swapping balls, players move on to 1v1's. Remove half the balls and get the players to practise 1v1's in the circle.

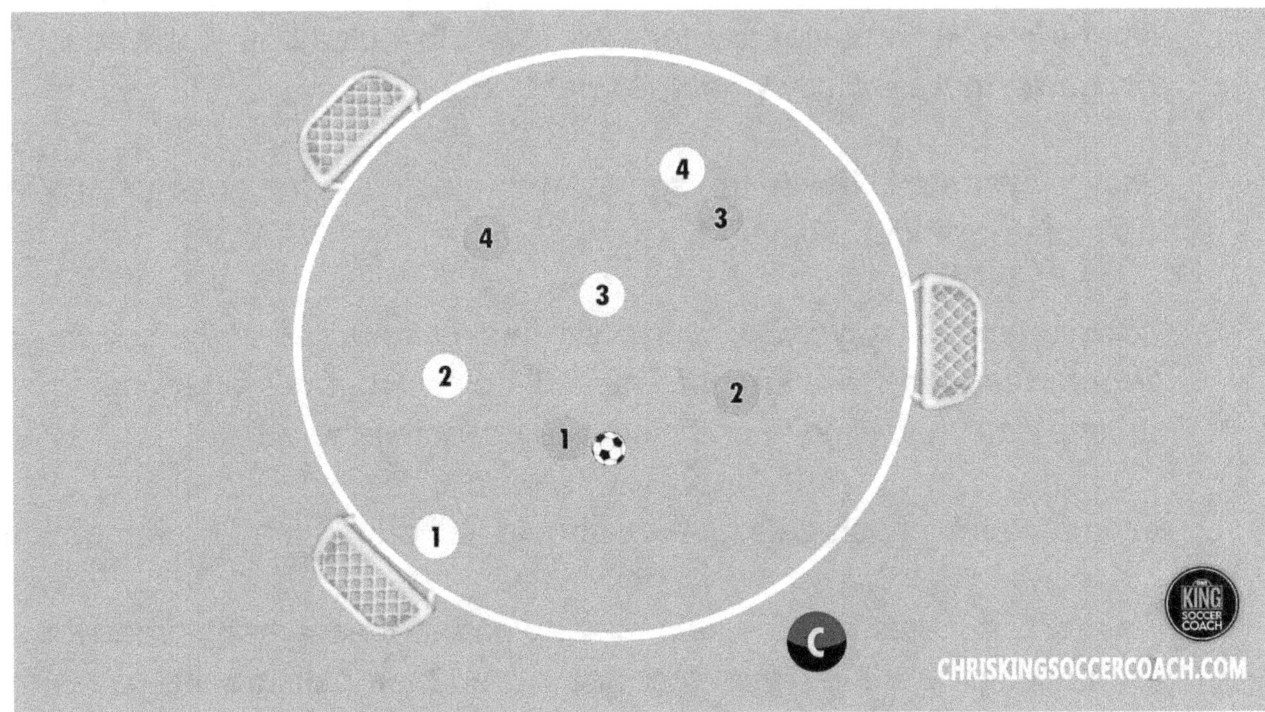

Lastly, split the players into two teams and play a game where they can use all the skills they've just been practising. They can score in any goal.

GAME #7
"OUCH"

 FOCUS OF SESSION:

To encourage the kids to get their heads up while they dribble. This helps them to become aware of where the options are to pass and where the Defenders are.

This drill also helps with striking at a target.

SET UP:

- **5 to 12 players + at least 1 Coach (or parent)!**
- 20x20 yard square

What more can a player ask for than to get to kick a ball at the coach? In this game that's exactly what they get to do!

Each player starts inside the square with a ball and the coach starts inside the square without a ball.

When the coach says "Go!" players get to kick the ball at the coach - *aiming for below the knees!* This drill helps with the players being able to strike a ball on the move and also with scanning the area.

Each time the coach gets hit they should yell out "Ouch!" or something silly.

Play for 2 minutes, get the kids to keep count of how many times they have hit the coach and the player that has kicked their ball into the coach the most gets a high five from all the players.

- Make sure to say that it has to be below the knee for it to count.

- The coach should change directions, dodge and weave so that the players have to look up to see where they are.

- Show the players the correct technique for passing/striking a ball: Eyes up to look at the target and then eyes back down on the ball to strike it. If it's a close range shot, it can be a pass with the instep. But if it's longer range, show them how to shoot with the laces to get more power.

#1 - If the kids are struggling to hit the coach, slow down and stay in one spot for a second or two to make it easier for them.

#2 - Can players use both feet to dribble and shoot?

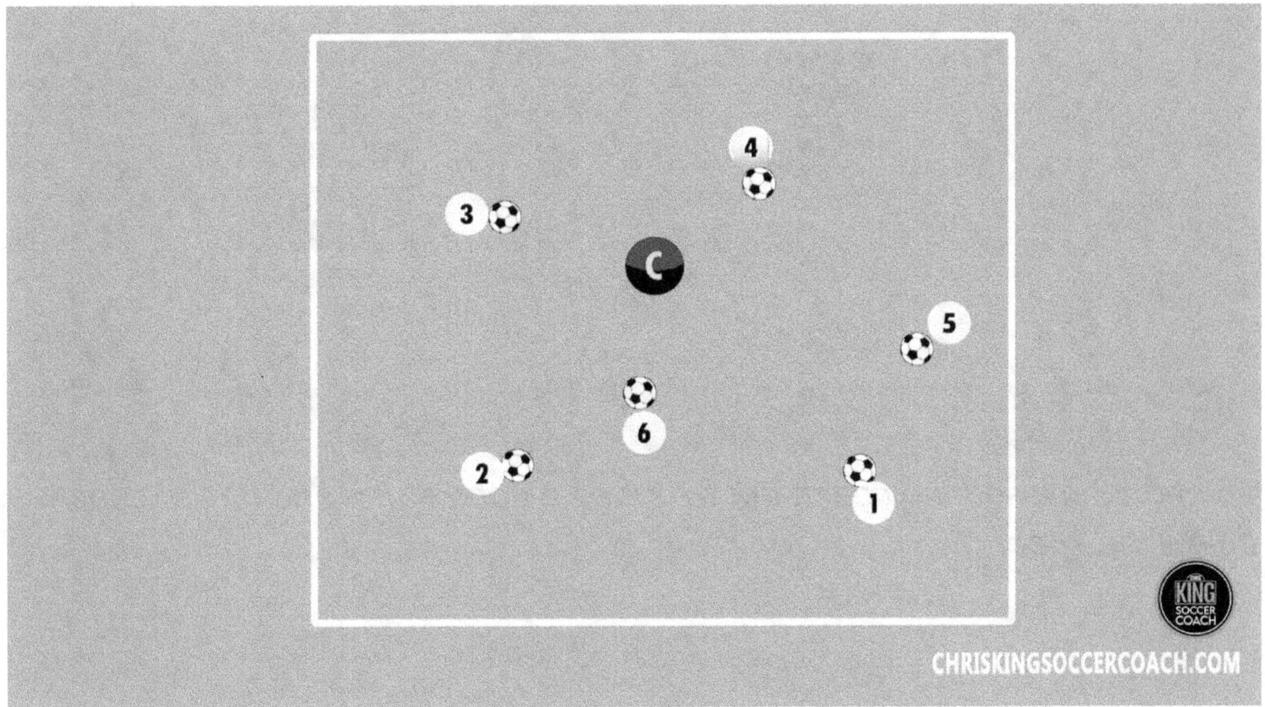

All the players start inside the square with a ball each. Once the coach says "Go!" the coach starts dodging around the square and the players get to pass/strike the ball into the coach (below the knee!).

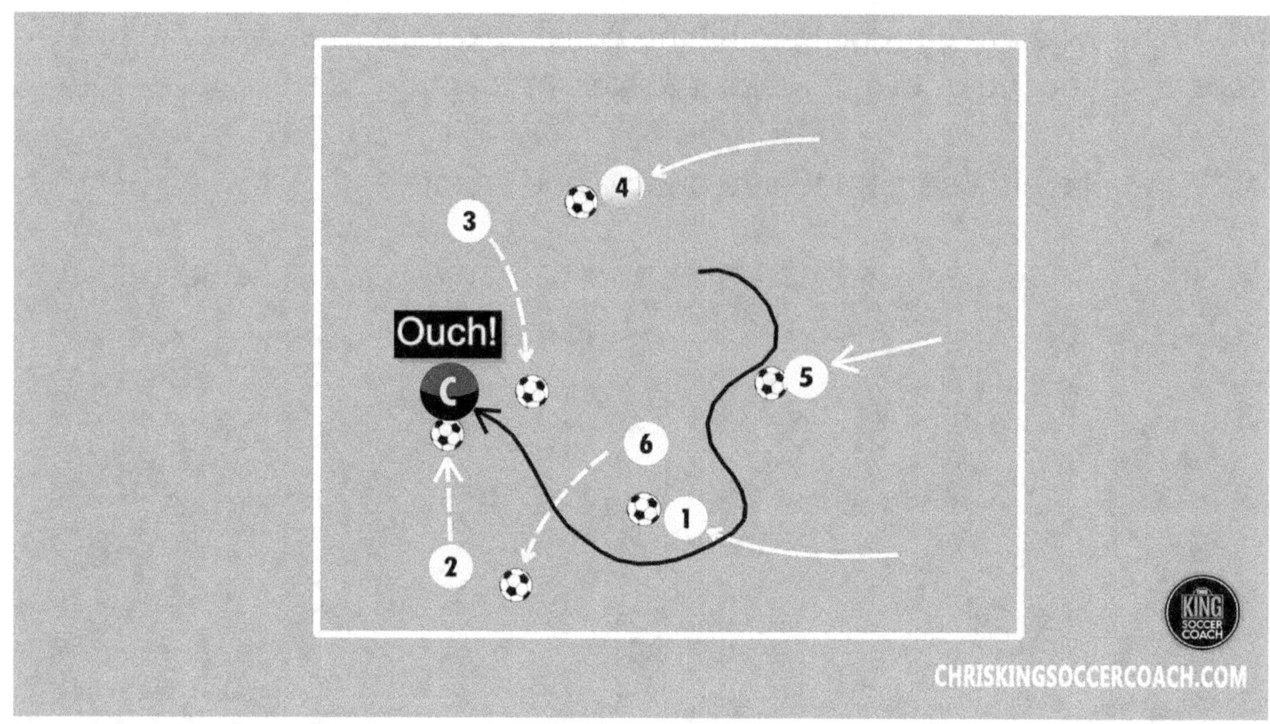

#6 and #3 missed the coach but #2's was a good strike and hit the coach below the knee!

GAME #8
"1v1"

⬤ FOCUS OF SESSION:

Good ball control so as to be able to beat an opponent 1v1.

⬛ SET UP:

- **6 to 10 players**
- 35x30 yard rectangle
- 6 mini goals

THE DRILL:

Set up a large rectangle (approx 35x30 yards). Place 3 mini goals at each end.

Pair the players up, start at opposite ends with one player with a ball.

The Defender passes the ball to the Attacker who takes control and tries to beat the Defender and score in the goal closest to them at the other end.

If the Defender wins the ball they can try and score in the goal at the opposite end.

Swap roles after each turn.

Note: *Make sure to limit each go to approximately 10-20 seconds. We want to encourage the players to go at the Defender, as opposed to stopping, going back, shielding the ball, etc.*

COACHES NOTES:

- Make sure the players keep close control. They may want to dribble too fast but they need to keep it under control, otherwise it is easy for the Defender to win the ball. If they have lots of space in front of them they can take longer strides/touches (i.e. have more than 1 step in between each touch). But when the Defender is closer they should be shorter touches (one step for every touch) so they can change direction easily and keep it away from the Defender.

- The Attacker should get their heads up as much as possible so they are away of where the Defender is. They should use different parts of the foot to change direction and get past the Defender.

- Different speeds can also help in getting past opponents. If they send the Defender one way with a feint, can they speed off the other direction?

CHANGE IT:

- Team players up and play 2v2.

- Team all the players up into two teams and play against each other.

- If you don't have enough space or players are getting tired, have 2 pairs behind each other and take it in turns.

- Set up a cone for the players to practise against before moving on to a real 1v1 situation.

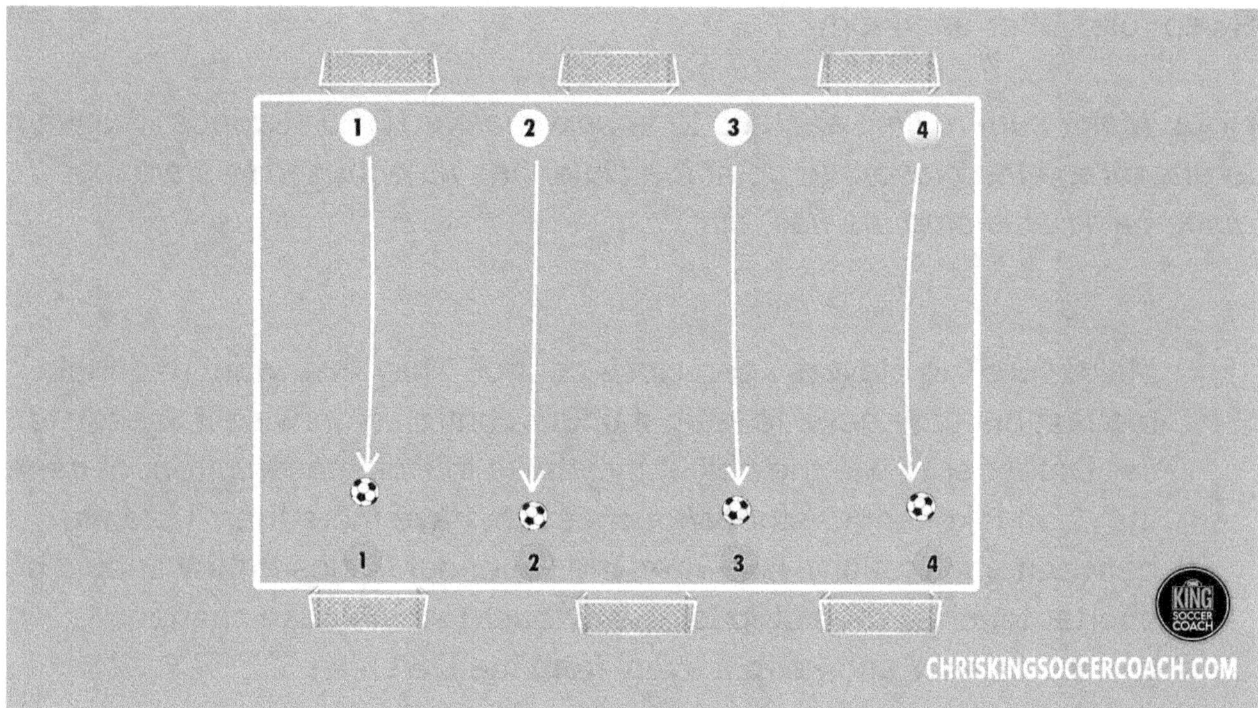

Players get to practise 1v1 situations. Defenders (Light) start with the ball and pass the ball to the Attackers (Dark) to start play.

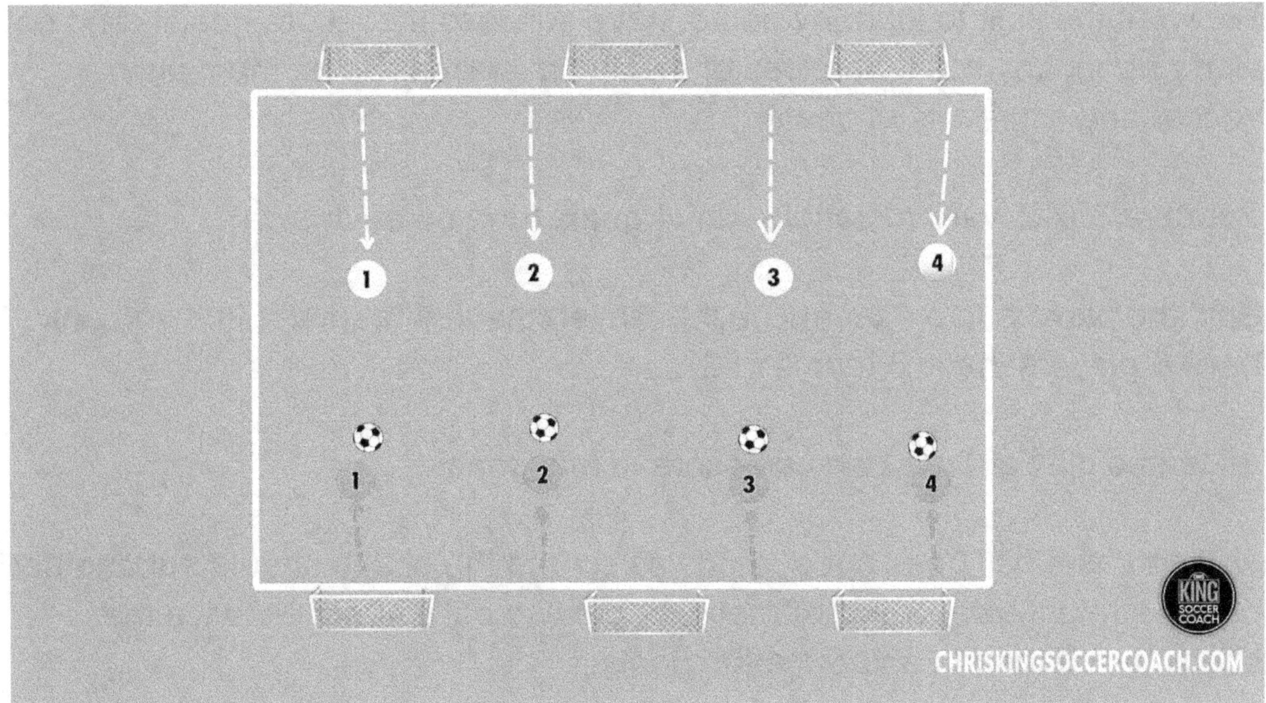

Defenders get out to the Attackers as fast as they can to shut them down. Attackers get to practise feints, shoulders drops, going at pace, etc to get past their Defender and score in the goal. Swap after each go.

GAME #9
"4 GOAL FUN SOCCER"

● FOCUS OF SESSION:

Let the kids learn by playing - just play soccer and have fun like they would at lunchtime at school. All skills will be worked on naturally.

■ SET UP:

- **6 to 12 players**
- 35x25 yard rectangle
- 4 mini goals

THE DRILL:

We want the kids to learn by doing, have success (i.e. score goals!) and not worry about any consequences of making mistakes. So let them play soccer and score lots of goals!

Set up a 35x25 yard rectangle with 4 goals (one on each side).

Split the players into 4 teams (ie if 8 players have 4 teams of 2. If you only have 6 players, have 3 teams of 2).

All teams play at once and can score in any goal!

As soon as a ball goes out or a goal is scored the coach should put another one in straight away. Also, sometimes put two balls at once! Twice the chaos, twice the fun and twice the goals.

The first team to 5 goals wins, then swap teams around.

COACHES NOTES:

- Make sure everyone is having fun! Lots of encouragement and celebrating when goals are scored (high fives, rolly pollies, etc!).

- Encourage players to dribble, pass, take players on and shoot. This is a great chance for them to work out how to do things in a game situation.

CHANGE IT:

#1 - Combine two teams (ie 4v4.). No need to even stop the game, just call out "Blues and greens are together versus yellow and reds."

#2 - Play 3 teams v 1. And if it's too hard for the 1 team, maybe the coach can join in and help them?

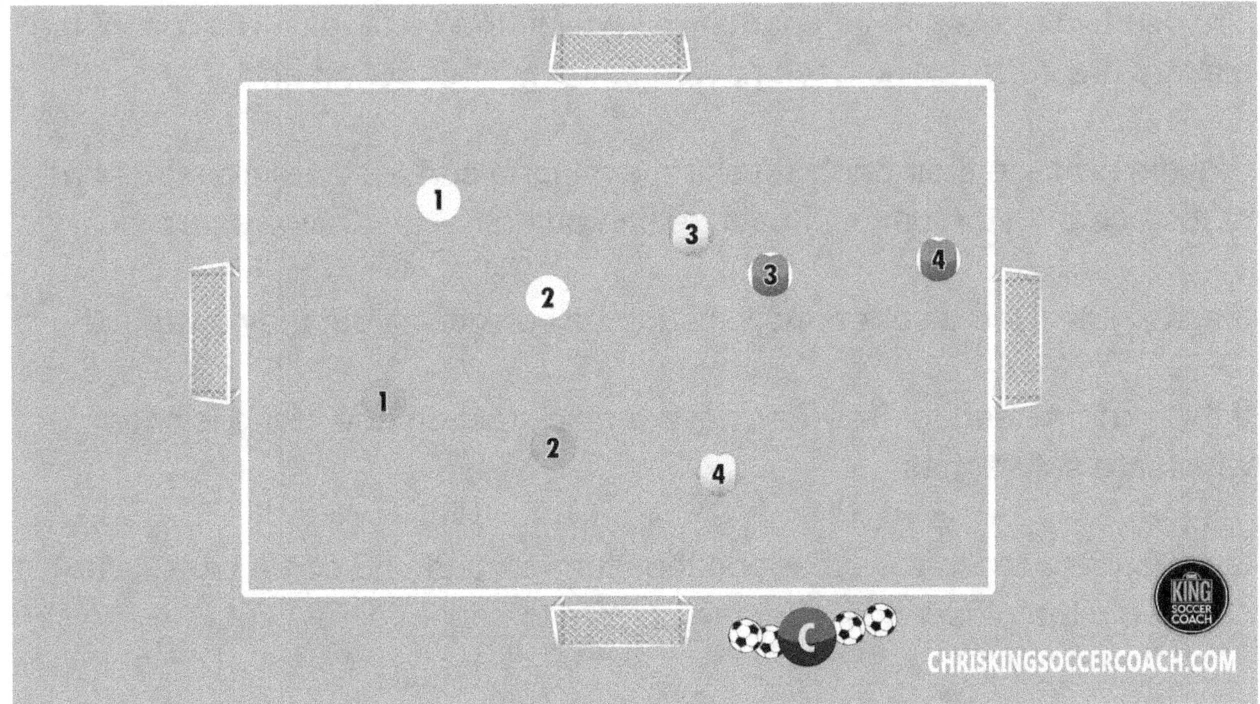

4 teams with 2 players each - players can score in any goal. This drill is all about having fun and scoring goals. Players get to practise all the skills they are learning (dribbling, passing, taking players on and shooting) in a fun environment.

GAME #10
"SURFERS AND SHARKS"

FOCUS OF SESSION:

Dribbling and tackling (and passing when using the progression change).

SET UP:

- **8 to 18 players**
- 35x25 rectangle with 3 different sized small squares inside the area

THE DRILL:

Choose two players to be sharks who wait in the rectangle. The rest of the players are surfers who each have a ball and start at one end.

Players practise their dribbling skills, aiming to surf (dribble) from one end of the ocean to the other without getting eaten (tackled) by a shark.

If a shark tackles a surfer and wins the ball or kicks it out they swap roles.

If the surfers need to, they can have a quick rest on one of the islands which are safe zones.

Once surfers reach the other end they turn around and come back. Who can get to the most ends? Get the players to count as they go!

<u>Note</u>: *Add or remove sharks if it's too easy or too hard for the surfers.*

COACHES NOTES:

- Encourage players to use different parts of their feet when dribbling (inside and outside of both feet and soles).

- Use a change of speed (or direction!) to get past the sharks.

- Stop the ball on the islands (this will mean that players should have close control so they can stop it when required).

- Shield the ball when required. Can they keep the ball on the other side of the body so the shark can't tackle and steal the ball from them? Players should keep their arms/elbows up to help make them bigger and keep the sharks away from the ball.

- Sharks should look to win possession as soon as they can. If they've just become a shark, encourage them to keep their head up and win a ball back straight away. This helps in a real game situation as they won't give up if they lose a ball. They will get in the habit of trying to win back possession for their team straight away.

- Make sure surfers aren't spending too long on the islands. If they do, bring in a 5-10 second limit.

CHANGE IT:

#1 - Add players (or parents) to the side and the surfers can do a one two pass with them to avoid being caught with the ball.

#2 - Add goals at each end. If surfers successfully make it from one end to the other they can have a shot at goal and receive a bonus point. Play for 5 minutes and see who gets the most points.

#3 - Team players up and give a ball to each pair and see if they can pass their way through the ocean without being eaten by the sharks!

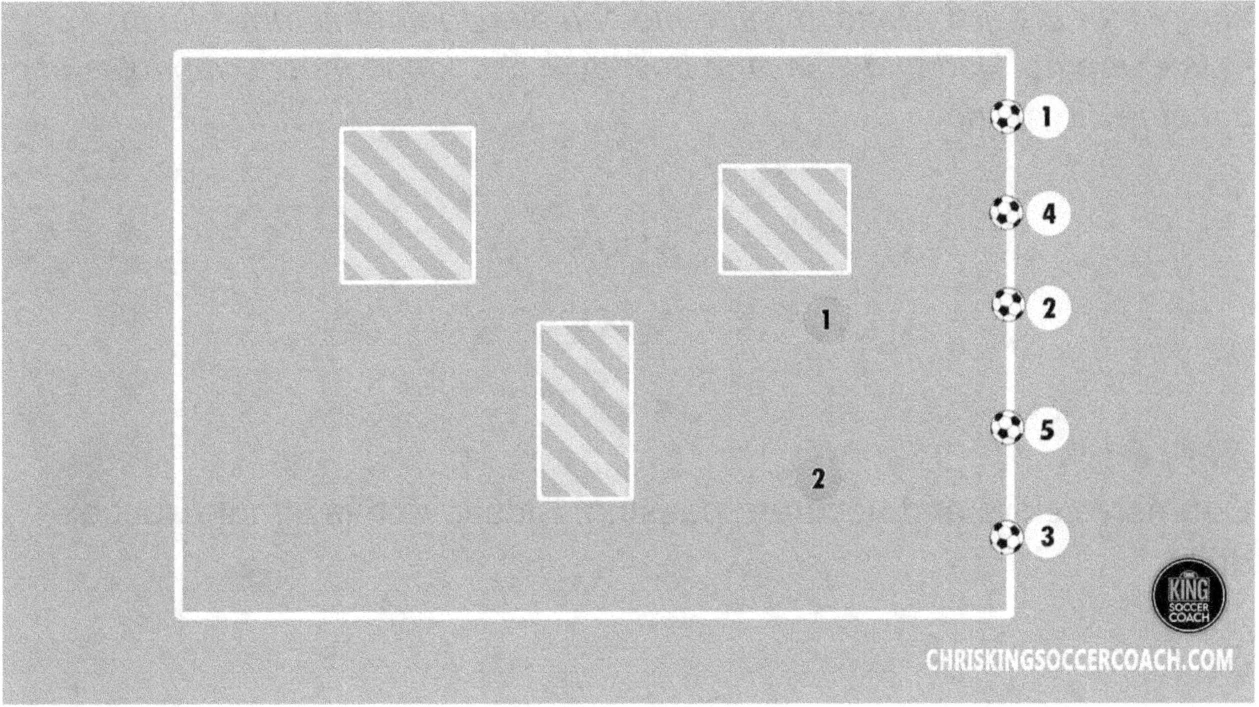

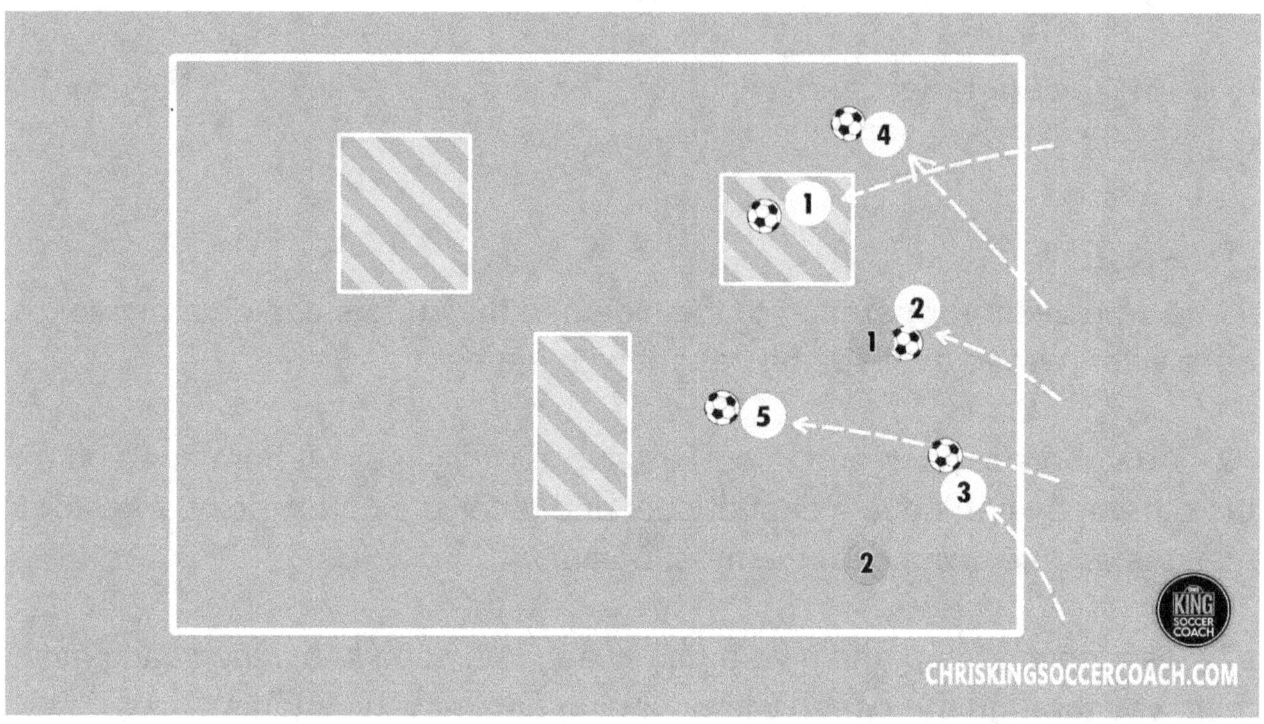

Light #4 is smart and goes wide away from the sharks. Light #1 goes straight for the first island, is safe and can plan their next move. Light #2 gets eaten (tackled and loses the ball) by a shark and must swap roles and become the shark.

GAME #11
"HIT THE CONE"

🔴 FOCUS OF SESSION:

Defensive skills and accurate passing. Kids love this simple soccer drill!

🟦 SET UP:

- **4 to 16 players**
- 10x10 yard square

Set up a 10x10 yard square with a tall cone in the middle (or a regular cone with a ball on top).

4 players per square with 1 player defending the cone and the other 3 passing the ball around the square and trying to knock the cone over by passing the ball into it.

The Defender must block any passes and kick the balls away to stop the attack on their cone!

Each round goes for one minute then swap the Defender. The Defender that has their cone knocked over the _least_ amount of times wins.

COACHES NOTES:

- If you find the Defender is standing right next to the cone, make it so they have to be 3 yards away from the cone.

- Make sure players are moving around the square to receive passes which will make space to have a shot at the cone.

- Players should have their heads up and be scanning the area so they know when to pass, shoot or where to move to.

- Defenders should be on their toes and ready to move, adjust and react as the ball moves.

CHANGE IT:

#1 - Attackers aim to knock the cone over 3 times. Then swap the Defender. Time the Defender to see how long they can defend until their cone is knocked over. Or get the defender to recite the alphabet as many times as they can as they defend the cone. How many times can they get through the alphabet before having their cone knocked over 3 times? The most alphabets wins!

#2 - Require the Attackers to make 3 passes before they can shoot at the cone.

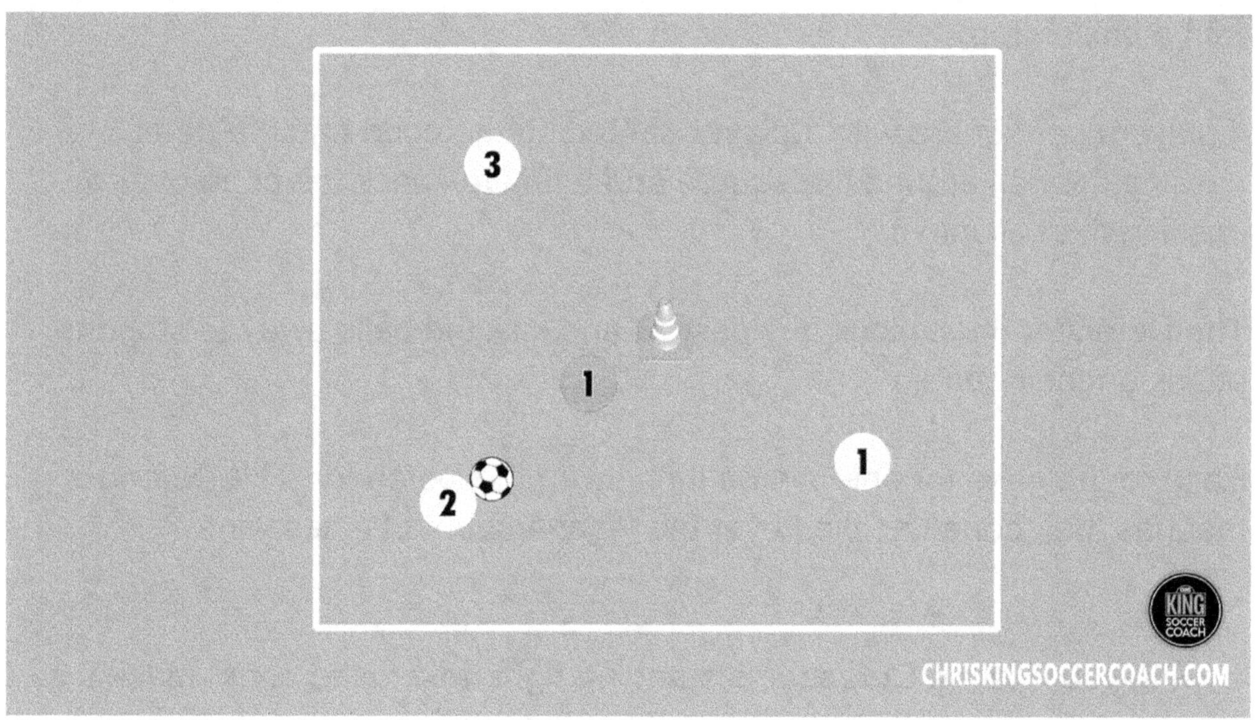

3v1 with the 1 defending the cone and the 3 aiming to pass the ball into the cone to knock it over. Play for 1 minute then swap the Defender.

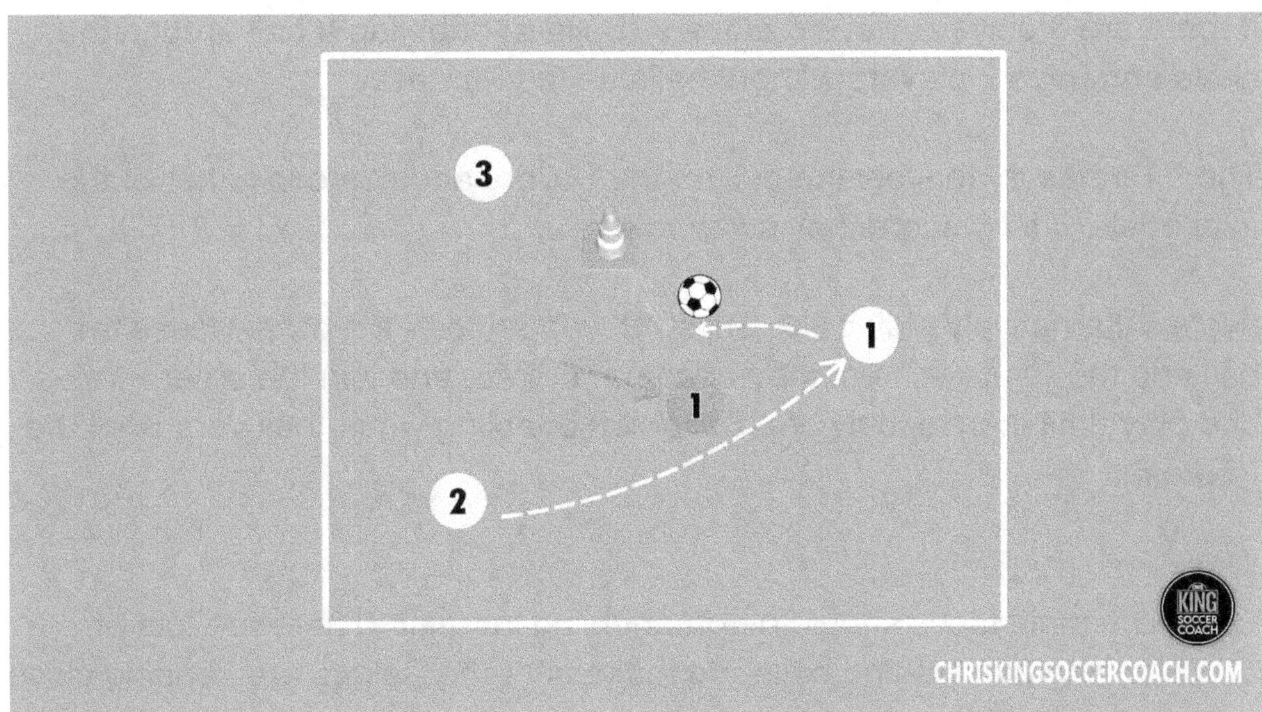

Light #2 has done a quick pass to Light #1 to move the angle of the attack. Dark #1 can't quit cut off the pass and Light #2 is able to knock the cone over.

GAME #12
"PIRATES AND SAILORS"

FOCUS OF SESSION:

Dribbling in congested areas plus tackling.

SET UP:

- **6 to 18 players**
- 30 yard circle
- 2 mini goals

THE DRILL:

Set up a 30 yard circle with 2 mini goals back to back in the middle.

If there are 8 players, have 6 players (Sailors) dribbling a ball around the circle and have 2 players without balls as the Pirates.

The 2 Pirates try to steal the ball off the Sailors and score in either of the mini goals. If they score they swap roles.

(Note: Alternatively play it like British Bulldog rules - if a player loses the ball and the Pirate scores, they become a Pirate and join the other Pirates and play until there is only one Sailor left dribbling with a ball versus all the Pirates!).

COACHES NOTES:

- The main focus should be on dribbling in traffic. There are lots of moving players and balls. So make sure the Sailors are keeping close control while at the same time scanning the area so they don't run into other players and can see where the Pirates are.

- Pirates should stay focussed once they win the ball so they can score a goal.

CHANGE IT:

#1 - If it's too easy for the Pirates, make the area bigger or have fewer Pirates. Or if it's too hard for the Pirates, let the coach join in to help the Pirates.

#2 - Keep the Pirates in for a set amount of time (ie 2 minutes) and see how many goals they can score. See who can get the most goals after all the players have had a turn at being Pirates.

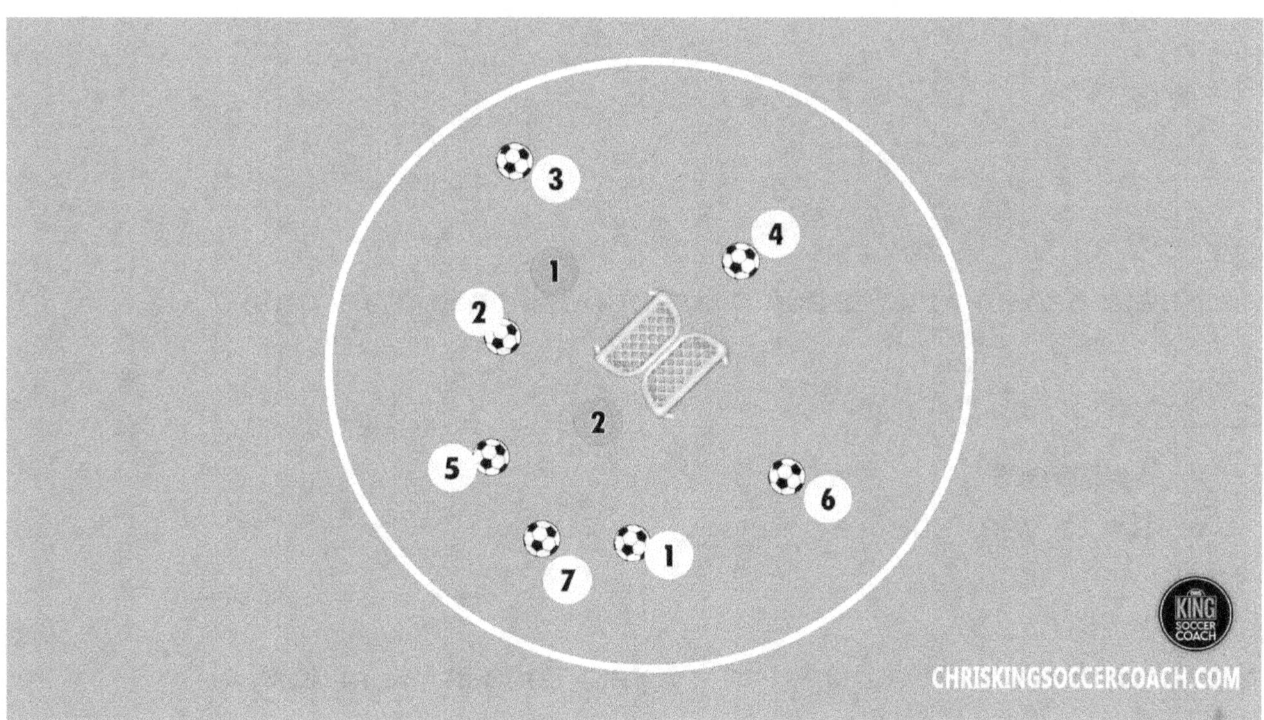

2 Pirates (Red) try to win the ball off the Sailors (Light) and score in one of the mini goals.

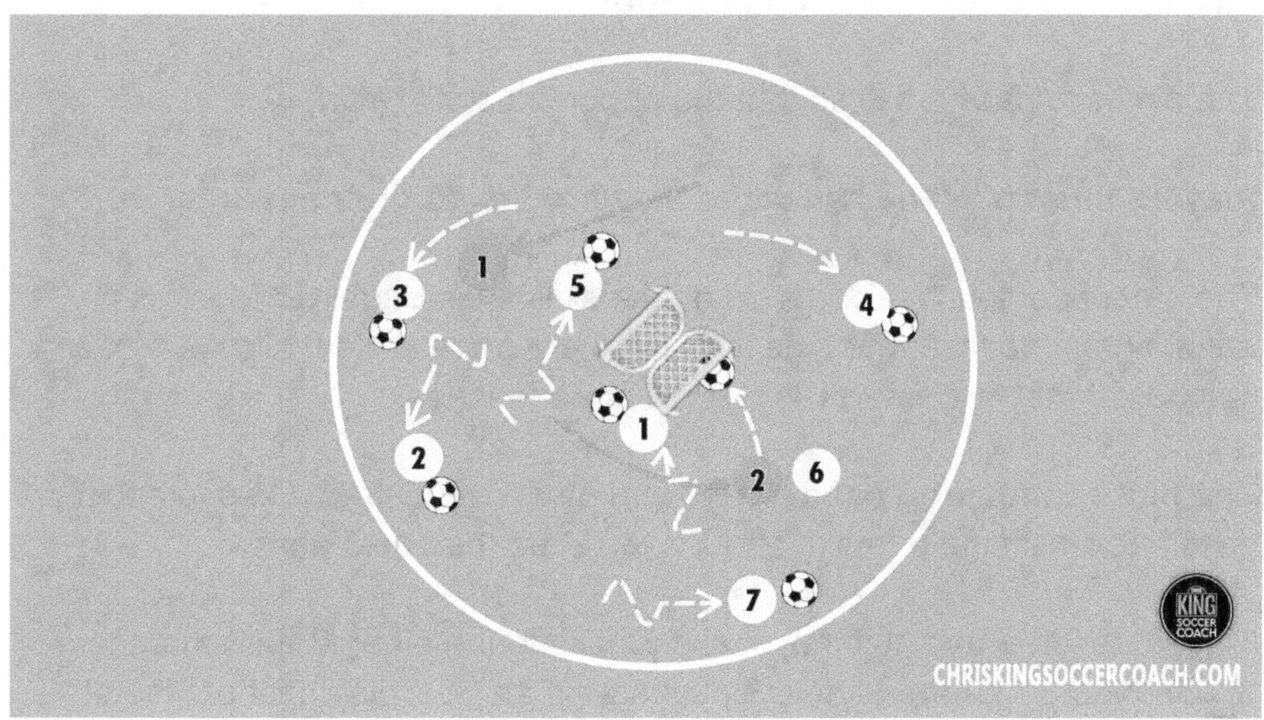

The Pirate (Dark #2) has won the ball off the Sailor (Light #6) and scored so they swap roles.

GAME #13
"1v1 PASSING GAME"

● **FOCUS OF SESSION:**

Accurate passing and reading the opposition's intentions.

■ **SET UP:**

- **2 players**
- 15x15 yard square

THE DRILL:

Set up a 15x15 yard square with a 5 yard zone in the middle.

2 players. 1 player starts in each square. Players must pass the ball back and forth to their opponents square and **the ball must either pass through or bounce in the middle zone.**

The aim is to pass a ball so that the opponent can't return it.

Players must play the ball while they are inside their square.

The amount of touches depends on the skill level. Usually 3 touches is about right for 5 to 7 year olds. If players are more skilled, allow less touches. If they are less skilled, allow more touches.

The ball cannot stop dead, so players must use their touches to either pass back first time or make a touch to set up their next pass.

Players receive 1 point if they make a pass to the other square that their opponent can't return. First to 5 points wins the set (play best of 3 sets).

- Unless the players are older and more skilled, encourage ground passing.

- Encourage players to pass away from where their opponent is. Or if their opponent is at the front of their square, pass it harder so they can't control it.

- Encourage the players to read their opponents intentions. Are they looking where they are about to pass the ball? Are their hips open and showing which direction they're about to pass? If players can work on reading the opposition's intentions they will become better defenders.

■ CHANGE IT:

#1 - Use just the weaker foot (this helps improve their weaker foot which pays off as they get older). Refer to it as their "other" or "non-preferred" foot.

#2 - Increase/decrease the number of touches allowed.

#3 - Players can return the pass from outside their square.

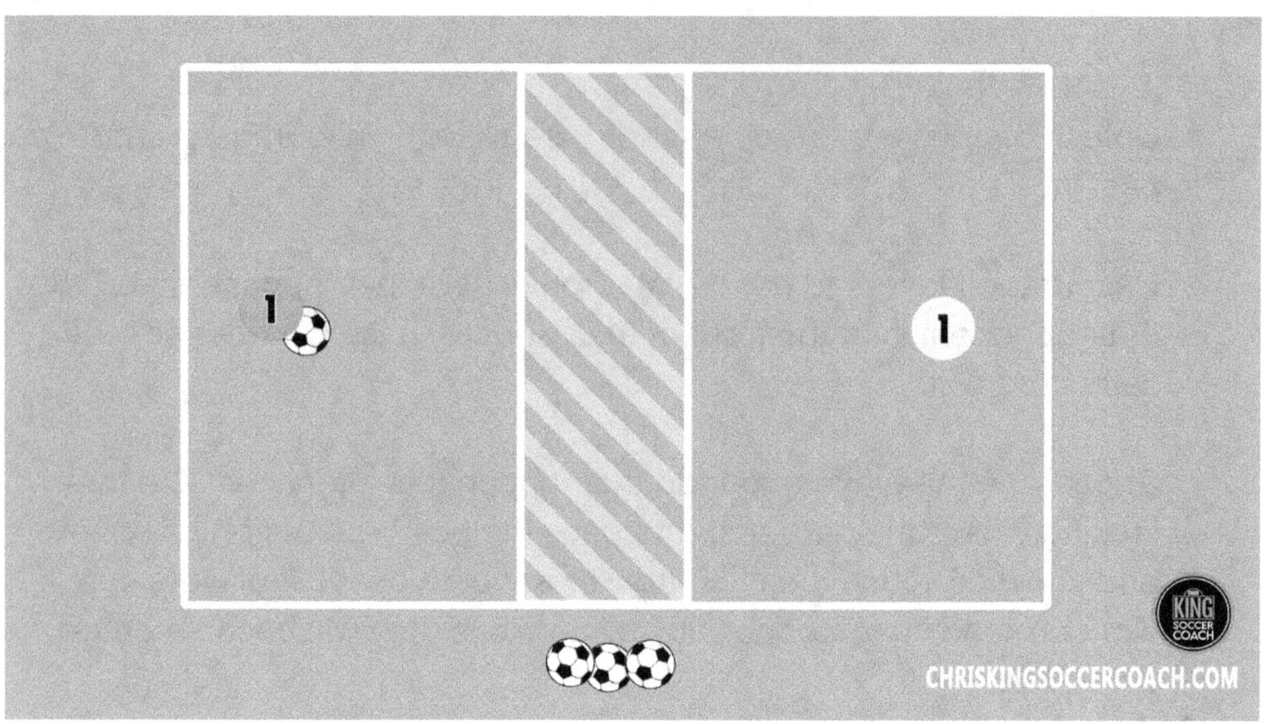

1v1. Players must pass the ball through the middle zone and the aim is for their opponent to not be able to return the pass.

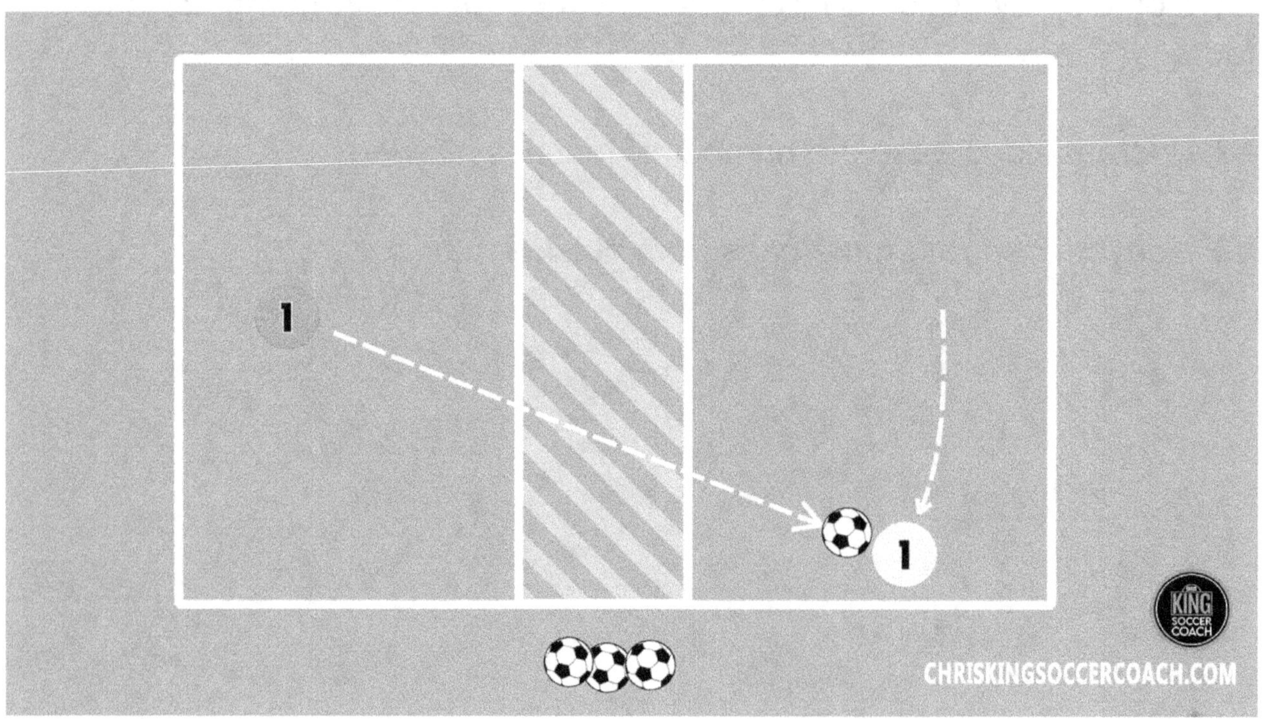

Light has read the pass and gets over to the ball. They must play it while inside the square.

GAME #14
"SOCCER GOLF"

● **FOCUS OF SESSION:**

Accurate passing and fun!

■ **SET UP:**

- **2 to 20 players!**

THE DRILL:

Each player has a ball. Play in groups of 2 or 3's.

Pick a target for each group (a goal post, a pole, a garbage bin, a tree, another soccer ball, etc). Players take it in turns of passing their balls to see who can hit the target in the least amount of passes.

For young kids, start each pass with the ball stationary. But for older or more skilled players can they do a skill before the pass? For example, can they do a sole roll (roll the ball with the sole of their foot) or a turn and then pass the ball?

Also, set up poles or other obstacles that the players must pass around or through before aiming for their final target. This will help them improve the weighting of their passes.

COACHES NOTES:

- Encourage players to "weigh" their passes nicely. Say to them "Do you think you'll need a small, medium or big pass for this one?". This will help get it clear in their head how much oomph to put into their passes.

#1 - Alternate feet with every pass (i.e. right foot for the first pass, left foot for the second pass).

#2 - Team up and pass on the move! Play 2v2 and players have to pass their way to the obstacle in the least amount of passes. This will help with teamwork and passing on the move.

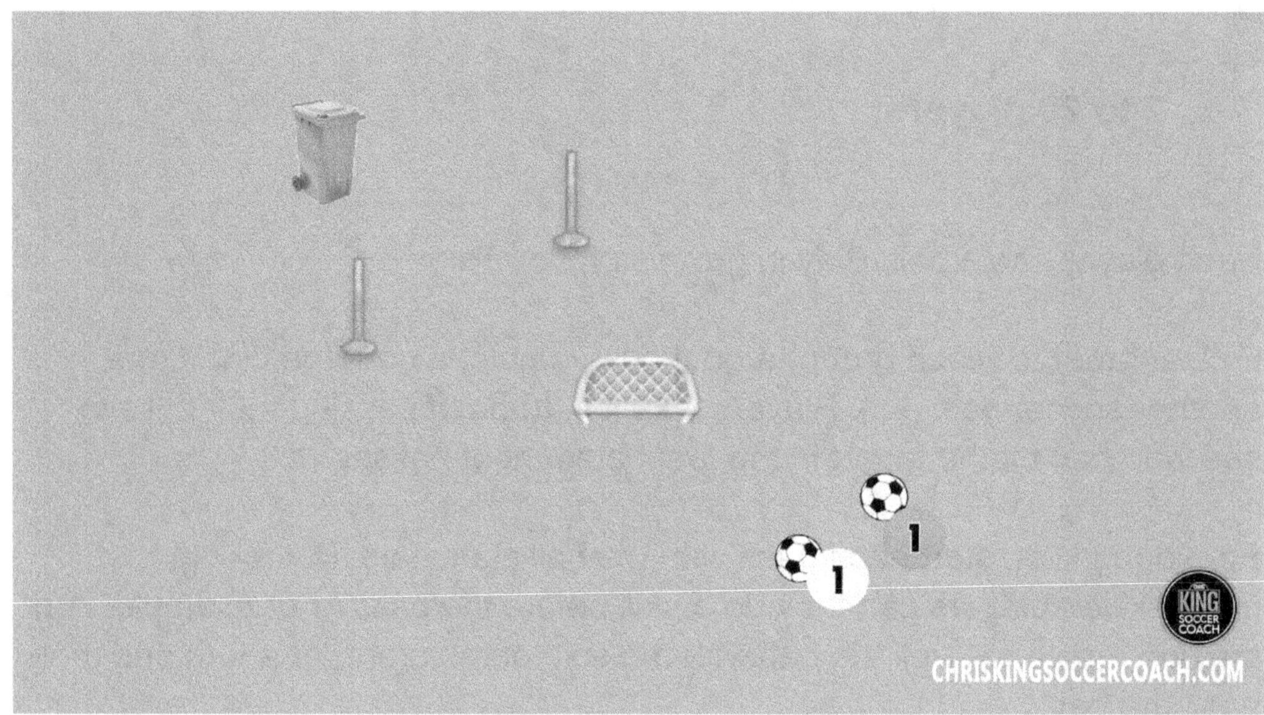

In this example the 2 players must hit the bin. They can choose which way to go around the mini goal and poles.

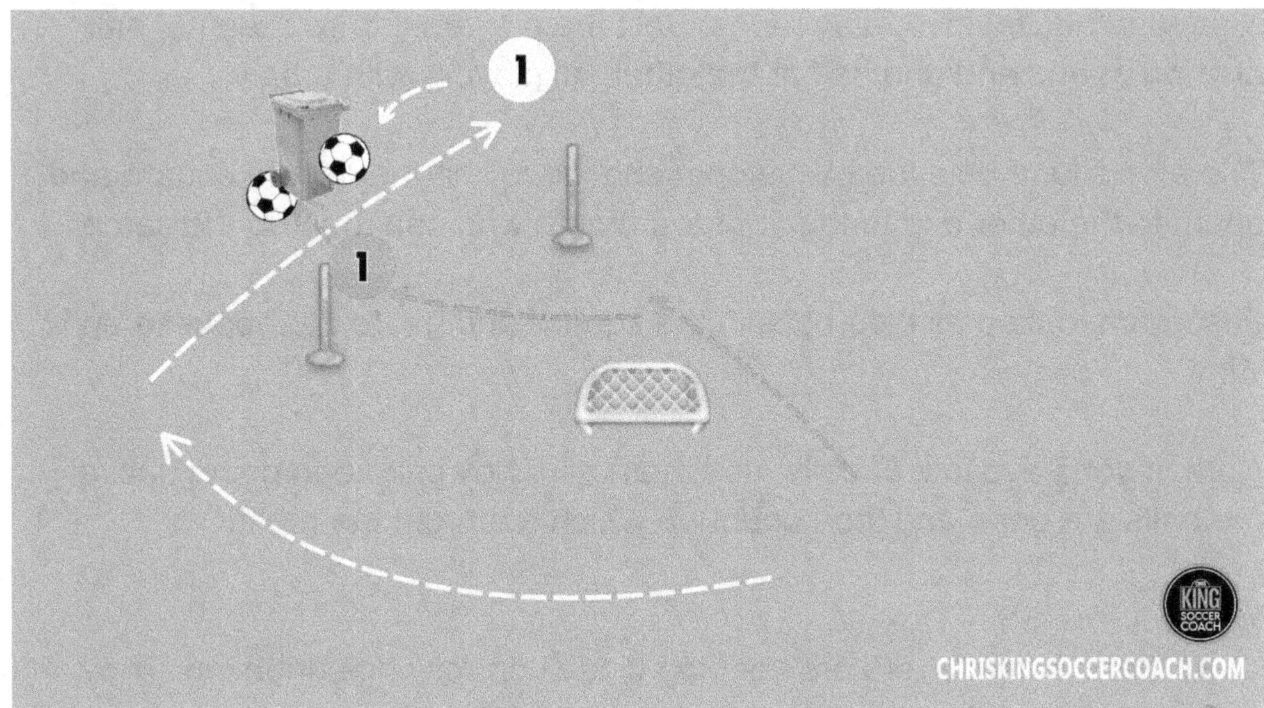

Light went left and it took them 3 passes to hit the bin. Dark went through the middle and also took 3 passes. It's a draw! 1 point each.

GAME #15
"FILL UP THE SQUARE"

⬤ FOCUS OF SESSION:

Dribbling and stopping the ball. This drill adds competitiveness and excitement to the session.

⬛ SET UP:

- **6 to 20 players**
- 40x30 yard rectangle

THE DRILL:

Set up a 40x30 yard square with two small 5x5 squares in the middle.

Kids (and adults) love relay races! Split the players into two teams, half starting at one end and half at the other, all players with a ball.

The aim is to dribble the ball, stop it and leave it in the middle square and sprint to the other end to tag your teammate who can then do the same.

First team to stop all their balls in the square and get to the opposite end wins.

Note: If you have lots of balls, use them all! They can keep going until all the balls are gone and then count up which team got the most.

COACHES NOTES:

- Make sure players are keeping close control while dribbling. They should be able to stop it in the square. As they approach the square encourage them to keep extra close control so they can stop it.

- Encourage the players to use the front outside part of their feet when dribbling at speed. This keeps the ball in front of them, they can look around and they can dribble faster.

CHANGE IT:

#1 - Relay race: remove the middle square and have the children dribble the ball to their teammate at the other end.

#2 - Slight variation: All players start at one end (instead of at opposite ends). They dribble and leave their ball in the middle square and sprint to the opposite end then the next player goes. Once all players are at the opposite end and sit down they win the round. High fives all round!

Teammates line up opposite each other, each with a ball.

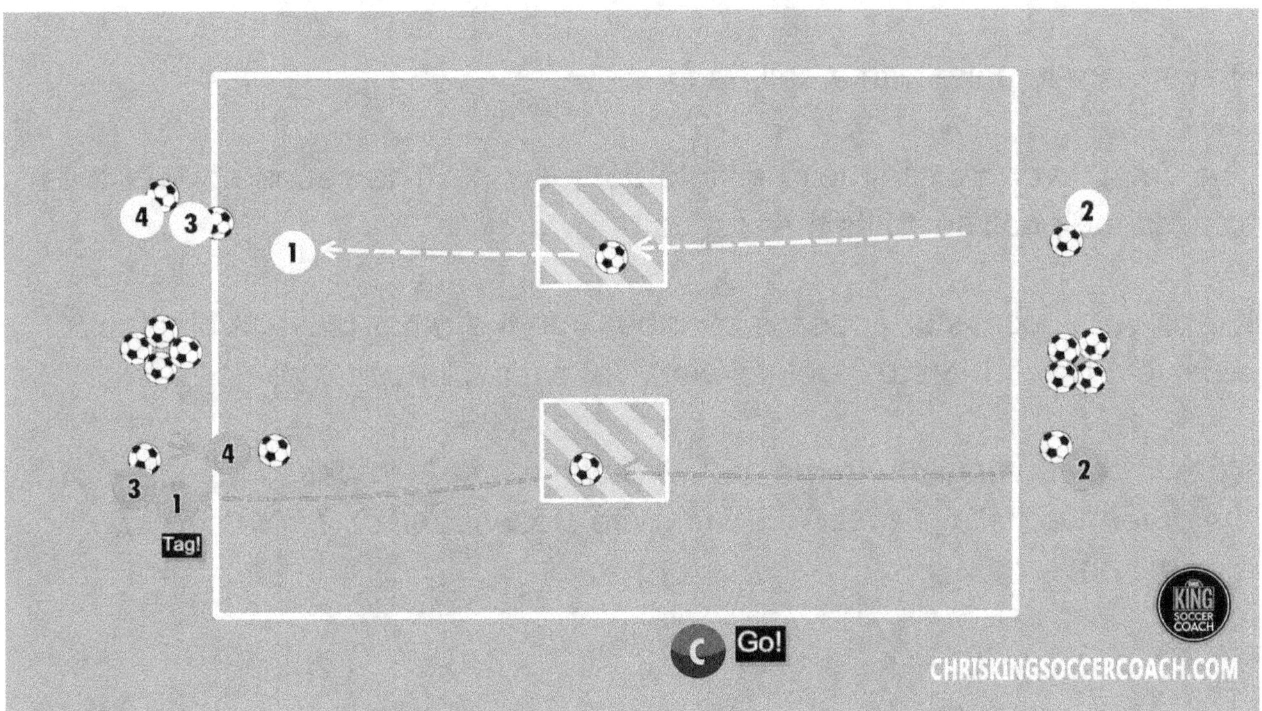

When the coach says "Go!' players dribble and stop their ball in the square and sprint to the other end. Here the Dark team is slightly ahead (Dark #1 has made it to the other end and tagged #4).

GAME #16
"MARBLES"

● FOCUS OF SESSION:

Passing accuracy.

■ SET UP:

- **2 to 20 players**

THE DRILL:

This drill is easy to play anywhere. If for some reason you aren't organised or need to talk to a parent or another coach for a couple of minutes, this is a good game to keep the kids occupied.

Players are in pairs with a ball each.

The first player passes their ball into open space. The second player tries to pass their ball so it hits the first ball.

If a player successfully passes their ball into the other player's ball they receive 1 point. First to 5 points wins. Take it in turns of who goes first.

Note: *You can play in groups of 3 with players able to pass into either of the other two balls (1 point for hitting the closest ball or 2 points for the furthest ball).*

COACHES NOTES:

- Make sure that players look at their target but then look down at their ball as they make their pass. Players should be using the instep of their feet to pass. This has the biggest surface area. Follow through in the direction of the target.

#1 - Players receive a bonus point if they use their other (non-prefered) foot and hit the other ball.

#2 - For young kids, start each pass with the ball stationary. But for older or more skilled players can they do a skill before the pass? For example, can they do a sole roll (roll the ball with the sole of their foot) or a turn and then pass the ball? This helps improve their ability to pass a moving ball.

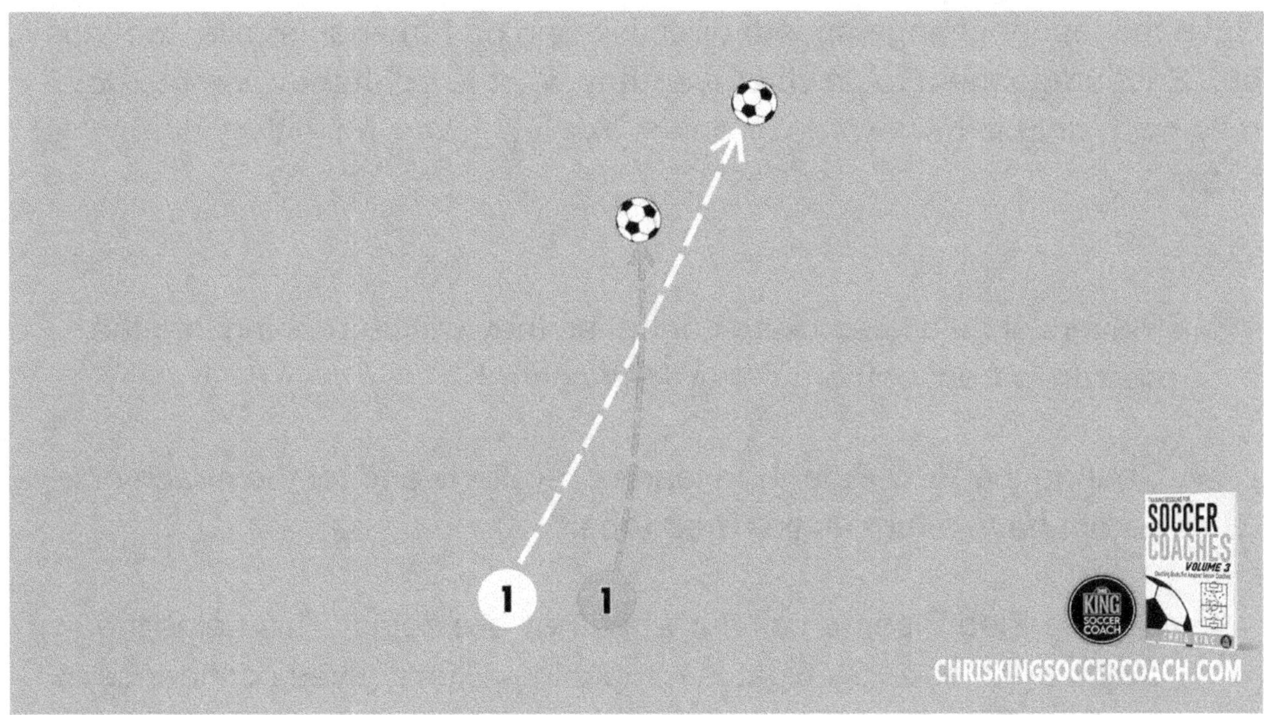

Dark has passed first. Light tried a nice firm pass to try and hit the ball but just missed. Now Dark will have a chance to hit Light's ball and receive 1 point.

GAME #17
"THE PIED PIPER"

Dribbling, turning and changes of speed.

- **3 to 20 players**

THE DRILL:

This is a fun, easy drill to start training.

Give everyone a ball and then pick a leader. All the players must follow the leader and do whatever they do.

Have the leader change speed, direction and do turns, sole rolls, toe taps etc. Encourage them to do whatever they want to do. If they want to do a rolly polly, dribble backwards or dance like a chicken while they dribble, let them!

COACHES NOTES:

- Players should keep close control as they will be running into the person in front of them if they lose control.

- Change the Pied Piper (the leader) regularly and let the coach or a parent have a turn as the Pied Piper.

- Get the Pied Piper to call out what they are doing. This helps the players behind know what is happening. Plus it gives confidence to the Pied Piper and gets them used to talking to teammates which is a key part of soccer.

- <u>Side note</u>: "Pied" means two or more colours.

CHANGE IT:

If you have too many players, make two lines.

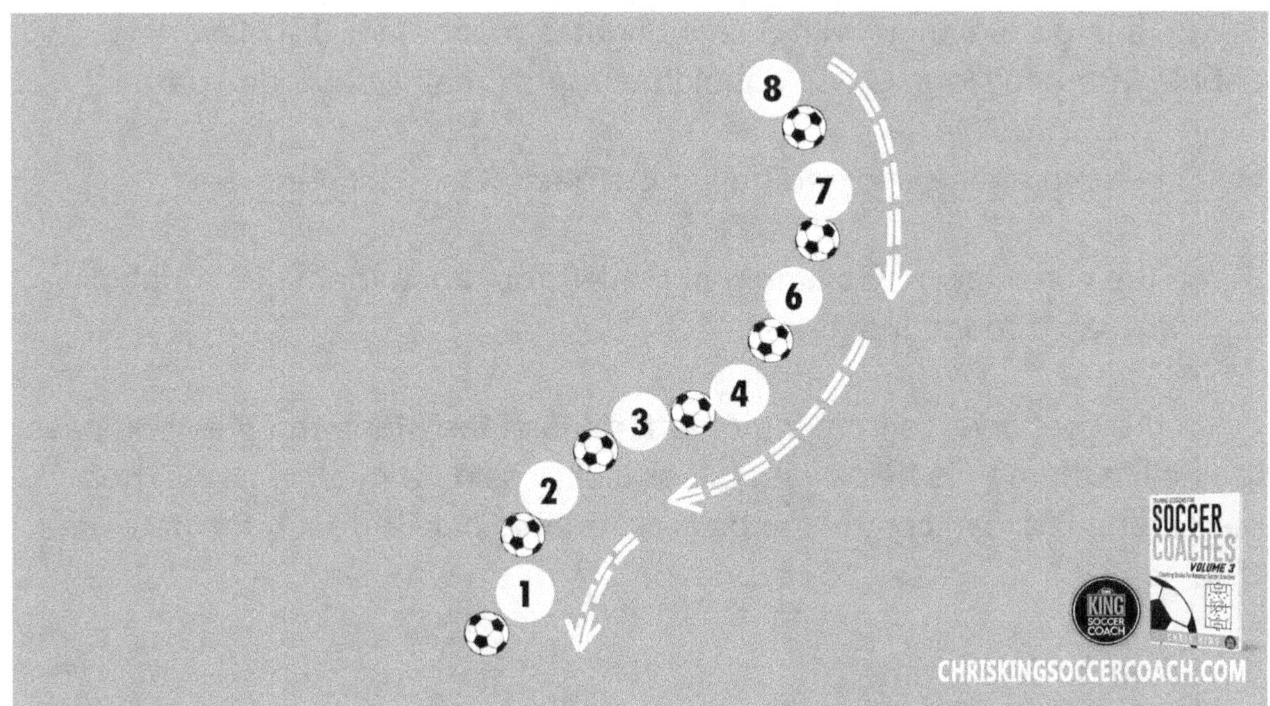

#1 is the Pied Piper and leads the rest of the players around the ground changing speed and direction, doing moves and feints that they all must copy.

GAME #18
"GATE RELAY"

FOCUS OF SESSION:

Dribbling, passing on the move, scanning the area.

SET UP:

- **6 to 20 players**
- 40x30 yard rectangle

THE DRILL:

Set up a large rectangle with 3 sets of gates (cones) for the players to dribble through. <u>Note</u>: Gates should be approximately 2 yards apart.

Half the team at one end and half at the other. One ball per team.

When the coach says "Go!' the first player from each team starts dribbling and must go through the gates.

Once they get 5 yards from their team mate at the other end they can pass the ball to them (this helps with the skill of passing a moving ball). Then their teammate can control the ball and dribble back through the gates the other way.

First team to finish wins.

COACHES NOTES:

- Encourage the players not to kick and chase their ball. Nice and close dribbling so they have control when going through the gates.

- Look for a change of pace - once a player gets through the gate can they show a burst of pace to get to the next one?

CHANGE IT:

#1 - Make the gap between the gate smaller or larger depending on the skill levels.

#2 - Have a parent (or another player) with two or three different coloured cones in their hands behind their backs. As the players are dribbling through the cones, get the parent to hold up one of the cones at random times. Players must call out the colour of the cone as they dribble. This encourages players to scan the area and get their head up while they dribble.

<u>Note 1</u>: You can make it so that the first player to see the cone being held up gets a bonus point.

<u>Note 2</u>: Alternatively, instead of cones the parent can hold up a certain amount of fingers for the player to see.

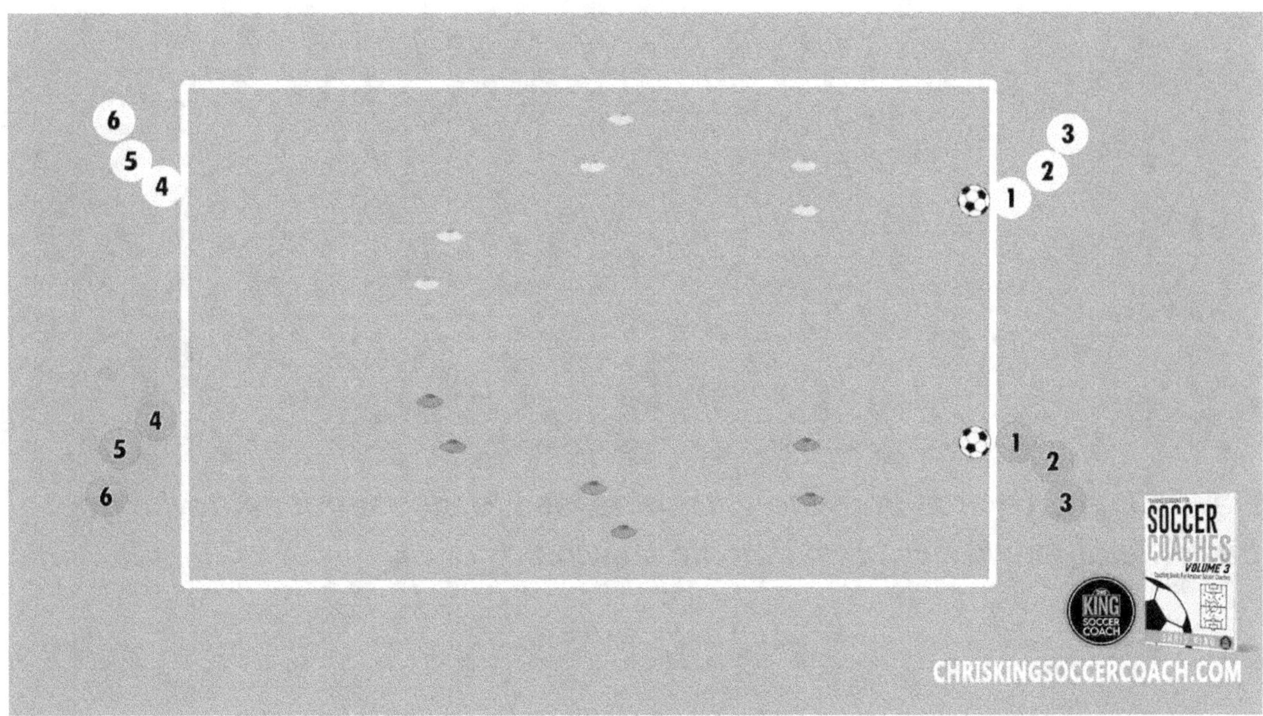

Half of each team starts at opposite ends. When the coach says "Go!" the first player from each team dribbles through the 3 sets of gates and passes the ball to their teammate at the other end.

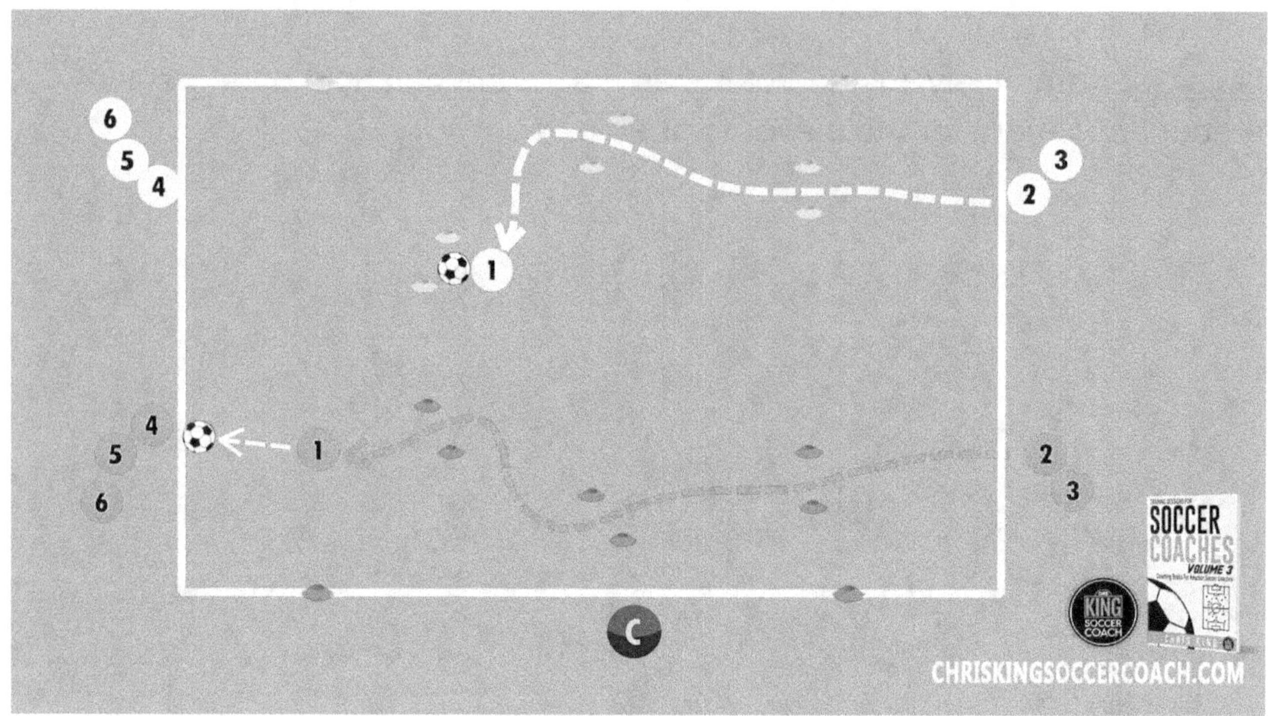

Dark #3 gets 5 yards from the end so passes to their teammate who goes back the other way. First team to finish wins.

GAME #19
"PARENTS v KIDS"

FOCUS OF SESSION:

Getting the parents involved.

SET UP:

- **4 players plus parents!**
- 40x30 yard rectangle
- 2 goals

THE DRILL:

Every fortnight or once a month, have a Kids v Parents game at the end (or start) of training. It gives the chance for the parents to bond and it gives the kids a chance to show them what they've been learning.

Make sure to have a quiet word with the parents so they know that the kids should end up winning ●.

If needed, the coach can play on the kids team to help encourage and organise them.

■ COACHES NOTES:

- Have the maximum amount of fun! Take the mickey out of the parents. There should be lots of high fives and smiles.

■ CHANGE IT:

Mix the teams so there are parents and kids on both teams.

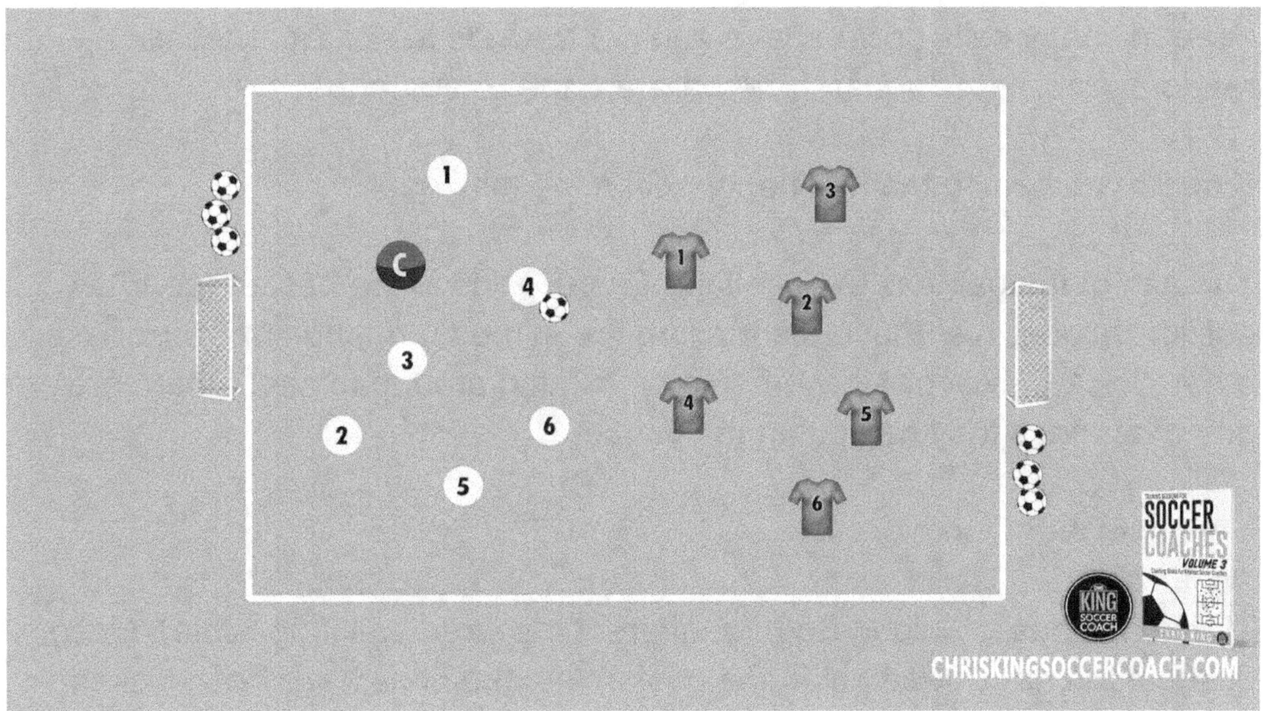

The Kids team (Light) which includes the coach versus the Parents team. Have fun!

GAME #20
"EASTER EGG HUNT"

Dribbling, shooting and maximum amounts of fun!

- **4 to 20 players**
- 30x30 yard square
- 1 mini goal

Set up a 30x30 yard square with a mini goal (the basket) at one end.

Grab as many balls as you have and get the kids to spread the balls randomly inside the square (the balls are the Easter eggs).

Kids line up behind the far line, opposite the mini goal.

The aim of the game is to get all the Easter eggs in the basket (goal) as quickly as possible! Players are all on the same team and can't tackle each other. Once they score they should be looking around to see if there are any other eggs they can put in the basket.

Here's an extra fun bit…

The coach has a Golden Egg! (a different coloured ball if possible). Once all the eggs have been put in the basket (i.e. the balls have been kicked into the goal), all the players go and hunt the coach who is dribbling the Golden Egg around the square. Whoever gets the Golden Egg off the coach and scores a goal can get the coach to do a small punishment (ie moo like a cow, roar like a lion).

- Just let them go nuts. Blow the whistle and watch the chaos begin. As long as they're all laughing, yelling and scoring goals this drill has been a success.

- If possible, time them and see how long it takes to get all the balls in the goal, including the Golden Egg. Then set it up again and see if they can beat their time.

Pair players up and they can work together. They must make at least two passes before they can score.

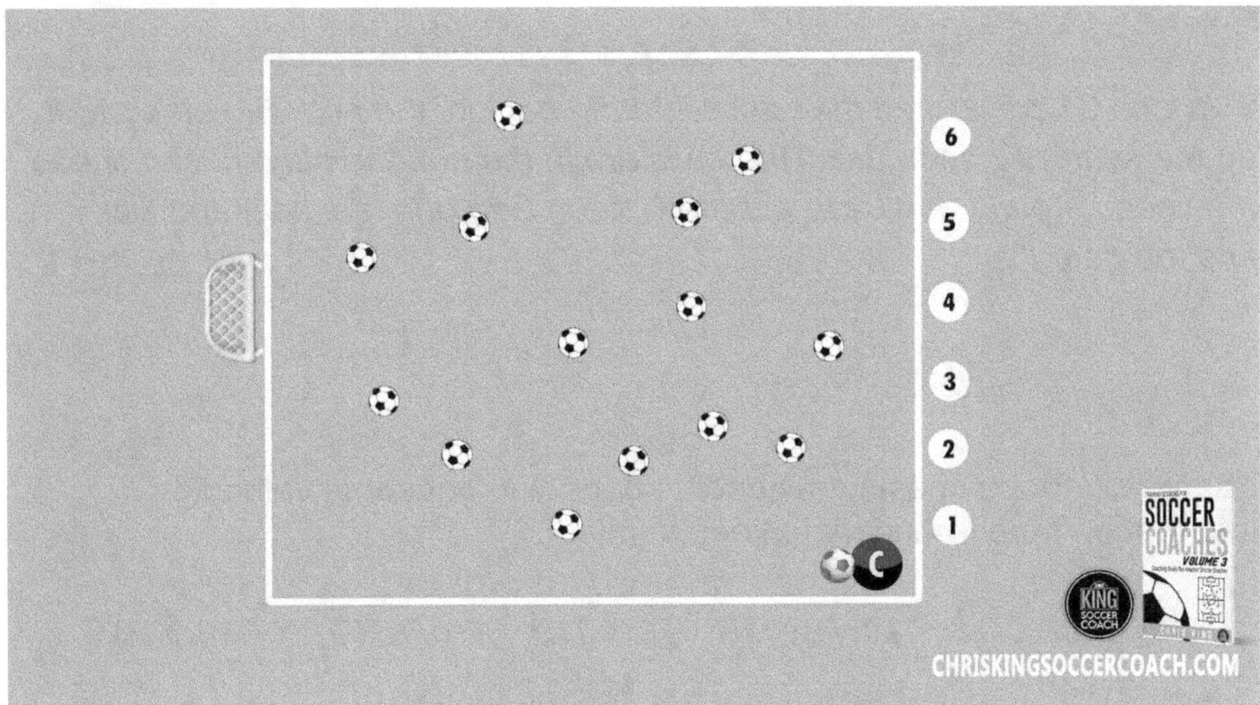

Balls are spread randomly around the square. The players must put all the eggs in the basket (kick the balls into the goal!) and then must get the last ball (The Golden Egg) off the coach.

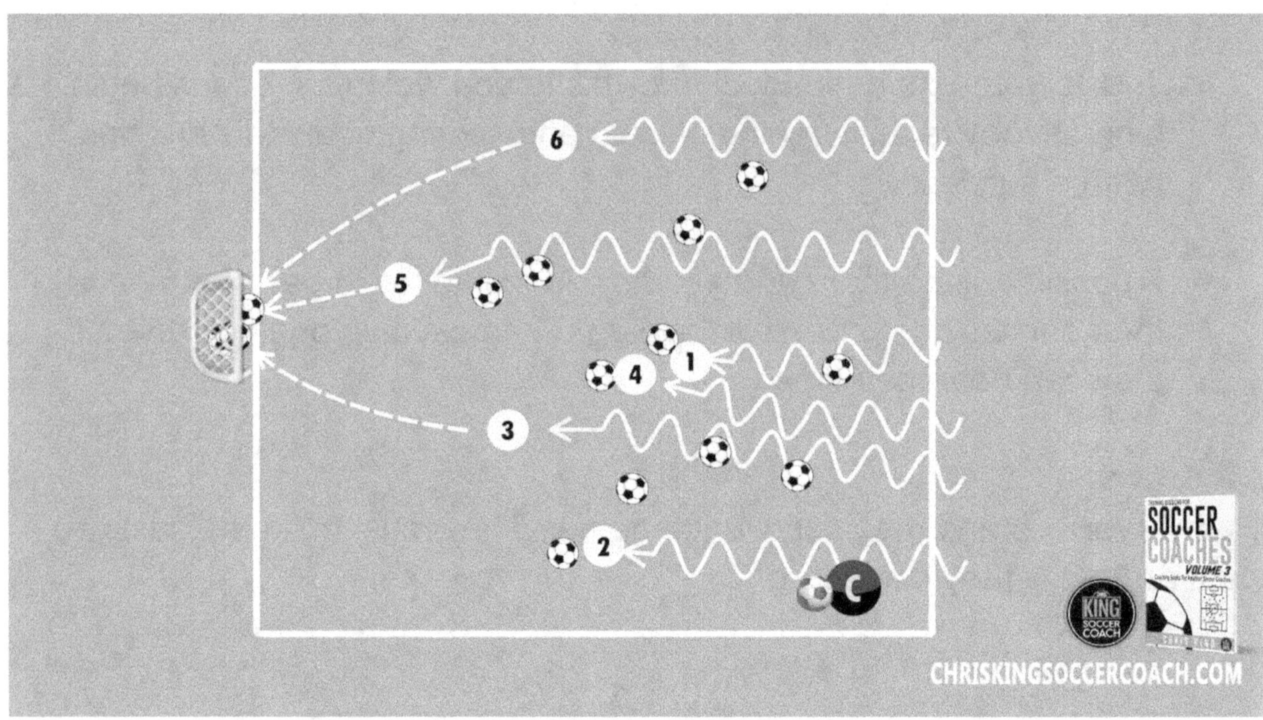

#6,5 and 3 have kicked their balls into the back of the net! The others will do the same. As soon as all the balls are in the net, the players can chase the coach around and try to get the Golden Egg (the last ball) and kick it into the goal.

Thank you for purchasing my book, I hope you got some valuable information from it. And try to keep in mind…

Every coach's main goal should be to help the kids have fun while developing their skills.

I also have a website that I post new drills and information on regularly.

www.chriskingsoccercoach.com

Thanks again and all the best with your coaching!
Chris King

And if you need "Coaching Kids Volume 1 and 2" or any other coaching books have a look below. I have full coaching sessions for senior players down to coaching kids soccer for parents or volunteers.

Just search for: "Chris King Soccer Coach"
Or www.chriskingsoccercoach.com

VIEW OTHER SOCCER COACHING BOOKS BY CHRIS KING
Training Sessions For Soccer Coaches Volume 1
Training Sessions For Soccer Coaches Volume 2
Training Sessions For Soccer Coaches Volume 3
Attacking & Shooting Drills For Soccer Coaches
Soccer Rondos Volume 1
Soccer Rondos Volume 2
Coaching Kids Soccer - Volume 1
Coaching Kids Soccer - Volume 2
The Ultimate Soccer Coaching Bundle Volume 1
110 Drills For Soccer Coaches

TRAINING SESSIONS FOR
SOCCER
COACHES
VOLUME 1
Coaching Books For Amateur Soccer Coaches
CHRIS KING

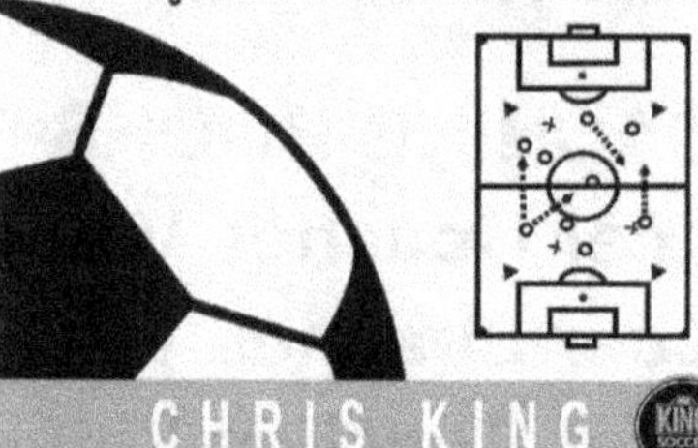

TRAINING SESSIONS FOR
SOCCER
COACHES
VOLUME 2
Coaching Books For Amateur Soccer Coaches
CHRIS KING

TRAINING SESSIONS FOR
SOCCER
COACHES
VOLUME 3
Coaching Books For Amateur Soccer Coaches
CHRIS KING

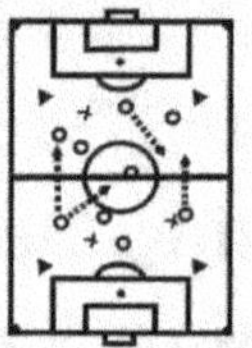

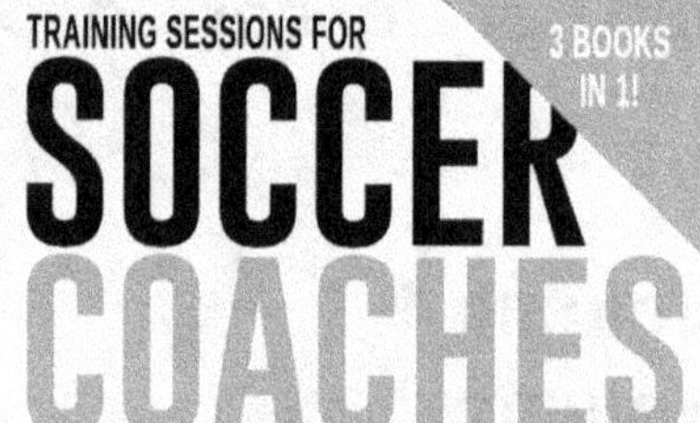

TRAINING SESSIONS FOR
2 BOOKS IN 1
SOCCER
COACHES
VOLUMES 1+2
Coaching Books For Amateur Soccer Coaches
CHRIS KING

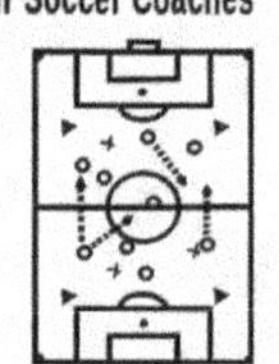

TRAINING SESSIONS FOR
3 BOOKS IN 1!
SOCCER
COACHES
VOLUMES 1,2,3
Coaching Books For Amateur Soccer Coaches
CHRIS KING

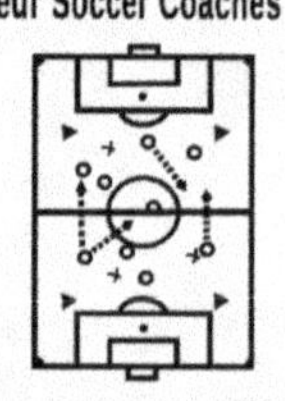

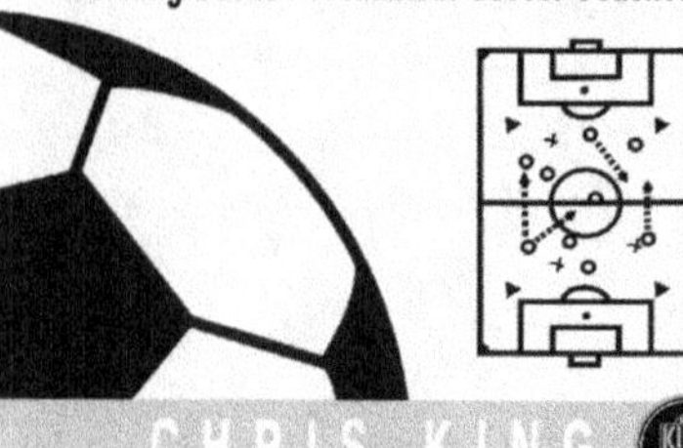

SOCCER
RONDOS
VOLUME 1
Coaching Books For Amateur Soccer Coaches
CHRIS KING

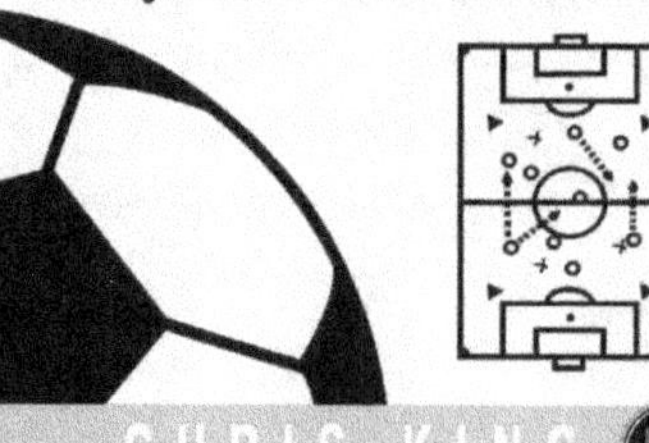

SOCCER
RONDOS
VOLUME 2
Coaching Books For Amateur Soccer Coaches
CHRIS KING

SOCCER
RONDOS
2 BOOKS IN 1
VOLUMES 1+2
Coaching Books For Amateur Soccer Coaches
CHRIS KING

COACHING KIDS SOCCER
AGES 5 TO 10
VOLUME 1
This book is for first time coaches, volunteers, parents and anyone wanting to coach!
Set up simple, fun and effective drills and organise a training session in 5 minutes!
CHRIS KING

COACHING KIDS SOCCER
AGES 5 TO 10
VOLUME 2
This book is for first time coaches, grassroots coaches, volunteers and parents!
Set up simple soccer drills that teach kids skills while having fun!
CHRIS KING

2 BOOKS IN 1
COACHING KIDS SOCCER
VOLUMES 1+2
This book is for first time coaches, volunteers & any would be coach
Set up simple, fun and effective drills & organise a practice session in 5 minutes!
CHRIS KING

ATTACKING & SHOOTING DRILLS FOR
SOCCER COACHES
VOLUME 1
Coaching Books For Amateur Soccer Coaches
CHRIS KING

5 BOOKS IN 1!
THE ULTIMATE
SOCCER COACHING BUNDLE
VOLUME ONE
CHRIS KING

7 BOOKS IN 1!
110 DRILLS FOR SOCCER COACHES
Coaching Books For Amateur Soccer Coaches
THIS BOOK INCLUDES 7 BOOKS IN 1!
CHRIS KING